7 SECRETS
TO INVESTING LIKE
WARREN BUFFETT

A Simple Guide for Beginners

MARY BUFFETT
& SEAN SEAH

Scribner

NEW YORK LONDON TORONTO SYDNEY NEW DELHI

Scribner
An Imprint of Simon & Schuster, Inc.
1230 Avenue of the Americas
New York, NY 10020

First Scribner trade paperback edition October 2019

SCRIBNER and design are registered trademarks of The Gale Group, Inc.,
used under license by Simon & Schuster, Inc., the publisher of this work.

For information about special discounts for bulk purchases,
please contact Simon & Schuster Special Sales at 1-866-506-1949
or business@simonandschuster.com.

The Simon & Schuster Speakers Bureau can bring authors to your live event.
For more information or to book an event, contact the Simon & Schuster Speakers
Bureau at 1-866-248-3049 or visit our website at www.simonspeakers.com.

Manufactured in the United States of America

1   3   5   7   9   10   8   6   4   2

Library of Congress Control Number: 2019017044

ISBN 978-1-9821-3033-6 (pbk)
ISBN 978-1-9821-3034-3 (ebook)

To all investors and aspiring ones

CONTENTS

Contents

Contents

SECRET 6: VALUATION

SECRET 7: PORTFOLIO MANAGEMENT

CONCLUSION

7 SECRETS
TO INVESTING LIKE
WARREN BUFFETT

The Lost Decade

You can't go back and make a new start, but you can start right now and make a brand-new ending.

JAMES R. SHERMAN, PHD

How different was your life ten years ago?

Did an event occur ten years ago that changed your life?

For some, a decade might seem insignificant. For others, a decade can be momentous. More than a decade ago, a young man in his early twenties lost $60,000 in the stock market. More than half of the money he lost belonged to his friends. He had convinced them that he could help make them richer with a "proven trading system" that he had learned in a business class. So, they entrusted him with their hard-earned cash.

This young man was Sean Seah.

Sean had been taught the risks involved in investing when he was a young man. He swore never to dabble in investments. However, he was dissatisfied with his financial status and started investing in the stock market blindly. Initially, he spent $5,000 to attend a short-term trading workshop and made an actual profit from his first trade.

He quickly gained immense confidence and invited his friends to let him manage their money. He raised $100,000 and lost more than half of the initial capital, in three months.

Sean was shocked but undeterred. After wiping tears of fear and disappointment from his eyes, he decided to take his investment education seriously and began to devour every investment book he could get his hands on.

One day, a friend recommended that he read a book titled *Buffettology*, which was co-written by the ex–daughter-in-law of Warren Buffett. He told Sean, "Using the techniques she introduced me to, my investment account has already gone up 60% since last year."

Sean searched for the book immediately. To his pleasant surprise, he found an entire series of books co-written by Mary Buffett and David Clark on the techniques and philosophy of Warren Buffett, including *The New Buffettology*. Sean studied the principles outlined in the books, and the young man who had once been clueless about investing began a journey that transformed him into one of the youngest investment millionaires in Asia.

MEETING THE TITAN

If I have seen further it is by standing on the shoulders of giants.

ISAAC NEWTON

Sean stood in the lobby and looked at his watch anxiously. "10:50 a.m. Ten more minutes."

He was so excited that he could hardly breathe. In a moment's time, he was about to meet the mentor who would change his life: Mary Buffett.

The ex–daughter-in-law of Warren Buffett, Mary had been part of the Buffett family for 12 years. She had listened closely to Warren and learned how he invested in the stock market. Mary saw many people step into the market with a short-term speculative mind-set. Not Warren—he invested logically, with intelligence and a fundamental methodology. And his investments earned billions of dollars.

Mary Buffett watched, listened, and began to absorb Warren's investing techniques and philosophy. In 1997, she consolidated her learning and coauthored her first book, *Buffettology*, with David Clark. This was the first of many bestselling books they published. Books that have been translated into 17 languages and distributed all over the world.

Sean studied and applied the principles outlined in these books to his own investments, and he quickly managed to achieve consistent, positive results. He was determined to learn more about Warren Buffett's investment strategy and techniques, and to meet Mary Buffett. After months of searching, he found someone who could arrange for a one-hour meeting in Los Angeles.

"Are you Sean?" a clear, crisp voice asked.

"M-Mary?" Sean turned around and saw a well-dressed woman in a pair of sunglasses. It was Mary Buffett.

"Shall we have some tea at the restaurant?" Mary asked with a smile.

After five minutes of introductions, investment ideas started to flow. Mary and Sean were completing each other's sentences and speaking as if they had known each other for years.

Their one-hour meeting ended up stretching from late morning till dinner. They exchanged numbers and have been discussing how to invest like Warren Buffett for the past ten years.

Mary has become a mentor and an adviser to Sean. With her help and support, Sean went on to make his first million in the stock market. His story was featured in the media and he gained fame. Initially, he started small private sharing on how to invest when his friends requested that he do so. These requests grew and came from more people. He then started teaching more regularly and has become an authority in the investment education field. Sean is now invited to top universities in Singapore, the Philippines, Myanmar, and China as a guest lecturer. Financial institutions such as UOB Bank, CIMB Securities, and Phillip Capital also invite him to share his insights in closed-door sessions. He is frequently interviewed on the radio and TV, as well as in newspapers and magazines.

Now pause for a moment and picture these scenarios:

What if Mary had never published any books about Warren Buffett's investment strategies?

What if Sean had never picked up *The New Buffettology*?

What if the meeting in Los Angeles never took place?

What if the book that you are holding now can kick-start your journey to becoming a confident and successful investor?

Mary and Sean decided to coauthor this book to help others learn how to create wealth like they have done.

As you read, you will find yourself having conversations with Mary or Sean. At times, both of them will share their experiences. So, do not be surprised if you see *I* and *we* being used interchangeably. Are you ready to turn the page and start a new beginning?

A New Beginning

Sean and I decided to coauthor *7 Secrets to Investing Like Warren Buffett* to explain Warren Buffett's techniques and philosophy to new investors.

The two of us are different in many ways. Sean was born, educated, and lives in Singapore, and has the perspective of the East. I was born, educated, and live in the United States. My perspective is that of the West. He is a man. I am a woman. We are from different generations. Despite these differences, our investment philosophy is the same. We want to share that philosophy with our readers and give them a chance to become truly wealthy.

The information in this book is designed to teach you

Warren Buffett's investment techniques and help you apply them effectively.

You will find two separate parts in the book.

In the first part, I will show you the habits you need to develop to become a truly wealthy person. Reading a book can give you knowledge, but it is the consistent actions you take that will change your life and your financial wealth. I call these consistent actions *habits*.

In the second part, Sean will explain how Warren Buffett uses the investing technique known as value investing to build his wealth. Sean and I both use the same strategy to consistently profit from the stock market. Sean will describe value investing in layman's terms so that even someone with no financial background can understand and learn to apply this technique.

Last, Sean and I want to encourage you to continue to learn and grow. As you grow, so will your wealth.

SECRET 1

THE POWER OF HABITS

CHAPTER 1

The Power of Habits

The chains of habit are too light to be felt until they are too heavy to be broken.

BENJAMIN GRAHAM

Habits define who you are, how you live your life, and the results you will get from your efforts. If you are overweight, it is very possibly due to not having the right eating and exercising habits. If you are broke, it is most likely because you are not practicing the right financial planning.

Truly wealthy people have habits that help them create wealth. But many people do not adopt empowering habits; instead they resort to get-rich-quick schemes, believing that one good investment, one jackpot, or one home run can change their financial destiny instantly and permanently.

On August 25, 2017, CNBC published an article stating that lottery winners and other people who receive financial windfalls tend to squander their newly found money and end up being worse off than they were initially.

Why is that so?

The answer is simple. It is akin to people who go on a

crash diet hoping to lose weight quickly. This may work in the short run, but your body is unlikely to maintain the weight loss over time. Most people eventually give up and eat more than they did before to compensate for what they've been missing, and they gain weight.

Fast results seldom work.

Warren once said, "No matter how great the talent or efforts, some things just take time. You can't produce a baby in one month by getting nine women pregnant."

What is the sensible path?

Take your time. Have patience. Be disciplined.

Remember, Rome was not built in a day. You can adopt sustainable and consistent actions that help you achieve your goals. Although results do not materialize overnight, the good news is that as you start to adopt good habits, you will be rewarded with small achievements. The key is to be disciplined and persistent.

In the following chapters, I want to share with you the important habits of wealthy and successful people. Adopt good habits, and you will start noticing positive changes in your life.

CHAPTER 2

Watch Your Spending

WARREN'S OLD CAR

Warren once shared an interesting story with me. For many years, he drove an old Volkswagen Beetle. People knew he could afford a new car and thought that the reason he kept driving the old was that he was cheap.

Rather than being offended by their opinion, Warren said, "Look—a new car will cost me $20,000. And 30 years later, it is going to be worth nothing. In fact, it may not even last for 30 years.

"However, if I compound $20,000 annually for 10 years, it is going to be about $150,000. In 20 years, it will probably become $1.5 million. And in 30 years, it's going to be worth $9.9 million!

"$9.9 million! That's just too much to pay for a car!"

Warren habitually thinks about purchases in terms of how much the item will be worth in the future, when its cost is compounded. If you can adopt this thinking whenever you are about to buy an unnecessary piece of apparel or a gadget, how much money will you be able to save and compound in 30 years' time?

Which comes first? Savings or spending?

Warren said, "You know, most people spend first, and save whatever's left over. But in fact, what you should do is to save first, and spend whatever you have left."

Believe it or not, this small reversal in thinking can make a drastic difference to your life.

The next time you receive your paycheck, set aside at least 10% of it as savings. You can then spend the remaining amount with peace of mind.

Later in the book, I will talk about what you can do with the money that you set aside. For now, it's important for you to adopt the mind-set that every single penny counts.

Every Penny Counts

There was a time when Warren was in New York City and found himself in an elevator with some strangers. He was so famous that everybody in the lift knew who he was.

All of them couldn't help but notice that there was a penny on the floor, but no one did anything about it. Finally, Warren bent over, picked the penny up, and declared, "A penny! On my way to the next billion."

So, how do we find that extra penny?

Finding That Extra Penny!

When my son, Sam, was in college, I paid all of his expenses, including lodging and tuition. Every month I sent him a few hundred dollars so that he could occasionally go to restaurants instead of having every meal in the school cafeteria. But every month he would run out of money and ask for more.

One day I visited him at school, and while I was driving him somewhere, I asked, "Sam, what are you spending the extra money on? You have everything."

He replied, "Well, I don't know, Mom."

Before I could continue the conversation, he suddenly pointed ahead and said, "Oh, wait, can we just stop here? I want to get a cup of coffee."

I pulled over, followed him into a Starbucks, and watched while he bought a cup of coffee that cost more than $5.

Out of curiosity, I asked, "How many cups of coffee do you drink a day?"

"I don't know," he replied. "My friends and I stay up late most nights, so we buy Starbucks. Probably a couple of cups per day."

Shocked by his answer, I stared at him and replied, "If you're spending $10 a day, 365 days a year, you are spending thousands of dollars on coffee."

Once we got back to the car, I drove straight to a discount store and bought Sam a coffee machine. Then I went back to Starbucks and bought a Starbucks cup.

I gave the two items to my son and announced, "Make

your own coffee, son. Put it into this Starbucks cup, and you'll look cool."

Fortunately, Sam followed my advice and has managed to save thousands of dollars every year as a result.

BUILDING UP YOUR SAVING MUSCLES

In one of the workshops Sean and I conducted, a participant provided a very useful suggestion to help people start saving.

He suggested that we practice saving by taking a small step every week and progressively increasing our commitment. He said, "This is what I did. I saved a dollar in the first week. In the second week, I set aside two dollars. And the third week, I saved three dollars. By the 52nd week, my savings became $52 a week."

This method illustrates three important concepts.

1. Progressiveness

    Very often, people tend to set ambitious goals. If they cannot achieve their goals within a short time, they tend to give up. That is why it is important to start small in order to get the momentum going.
2. Increasing milestones

    One reason many people find it difficult to build positive habits is that it gets boring after a while. When something is new, people are excited about it, but they soon get bored with it. Eventually, when the excitement has passed, many of them just give up.

However, changing our goal every week makes us look forward to the next week as the challenge becomes harder and more exciting. It's like playing a game. As we progress to the next level, the goal becomes more challenging. This is probably the reason why people become addicted to games. Make saving into a game and become addicted to it!

3. Consistency

With a better understanding of these three important concepts, you can apply them to help you build a good saving habit. The starting amount does not matter. What is important is to begin taking action!

Consistency is the key to building our muscle memory and turning something into a habit!

CHAPTER 3

Find a Job You Love

Take a job that you love. You will jump out of bed in the morning. I think you are out of your mind if you keep taking jobs that you don't like because you think it will look good on your résumé. Isn't that a little like saving up sex for your old age?

WARREN BUFFETT

If you were to map out how you spend your time while you're awake, most people would agree that they spend most of the time working once they have stepped into the workforce.

Do you love what you do at work? If you don't, you're spending a big part of your life doing something that does not bring you happiness.

Warren used to say, "Many people work just for money. As they don't love their jobs, their unhappiness builds up over time. Many end up bringing their negative emotions back home, instead of bringing happiness to their children and family members. So really, you have to be doing something that you love."

Happy People, Great Results

In many companies that Warren bought, the management stayed on because they loved their jobs. A great example is Mrs. Rose Blumkin, who is often known as Mrs. B. She sold Nebraska Furniture Mart to Warren when she was 89 years old and continued to work for the company until she turned 104.

In fact, she took only one vacation in her entire working life, and she hated it. During her holiday, she missed her job so much that she could not wait to get back to it. Under her management, Nebraska Furniture Mart grew exponentially, increasing its revenue year by year. That is the power of passion.

Passion does not just trigger happiness. It also increases our productivity. Passionate employees tend to achieve much more than unhappy ones, which often translates to greater financial returns. People who are happy at work tend to be promoted more quickly, earn higher commissions, and receive greater recognition than people who are discontented in their jobs. Granted, not everyone will get noticed for his or her hard work; nevertheless, your chances of being recognized will increase significantly when you inject passion into your work.

The Obsessed Tailor

Warren once shared a story about a tailor who was obsessed with his job. The tailor's dream was to meet the pope. He started saving money bit by bit so that he could travel to Vatican City and fulfill his dream.

One day, he finally saved enough for his trip.

When he returned from the Vatican, everybody in his community wanted to know about his trip. When the people said, "We want to know more about the pope. What can you share with us?" the tailor replied, "He's a 44 medium."

Clearly, the tailor had a passion for his craft.

Warren, too, is obsessed with his work. In fact, he is often so engrossed in his thoughts that he is oblivious to what's happening around him.

Once he and his partner, Charlie Munger, visited New York. As they were walking down a street, Charlie suddenly remembered that he had a plane to catch. So he flagged down a cab and left without saying a word. Warren didn't notice that Charlie had gone. He continued walking and talking to Charlie for two more blocks before it finally dawned on him that Charlie had left.

When he was away, his wife, Susan Thompson Buffett, decided to renovate the house as a surprise for Warren. She removed the carpet and replaced it with hardwood floors; she bought new furniture and repainted the walls. The first time Warren came home after the project was completed, he walked into the kitchen, grabbed his Coke, passed the living room, and left without saying a word.

As it turned out, *we* were the ones who were surprised, not Warren. So we approached him and asked, "Did you notice anything different about the house?"

He said, "Nope."

"The whole place has changed!" we exclaimed.

He finally looked around and replied, "Oh really? Oh, yeah, nice, okay."

Making Your Way to the Top…
from the Bottom

I want to encourage you to find out what industry you love and look for a job in it. Do not expect to get your dream position right away. As you undoubtedly know, most people start from the bottom and climb their way to the top.

Although an entry-level position may not pay a lot, it gives you the opportunity to start a career that you love. Many top Hollywood studio executives started out in the mail room.

The Passion Test

To help you discover your passion, you might want to take the Passion Test. On the next page, you will see four quadrants. In the first quadrant, write down at least five things that make you happy.

In the next quadrant, write down five things that make you angry. If you are angry about something and can determine why, it may be a chance for you to find your passion.

Next, write down five things that you're good at. Think of things that your friends may ask you for advice about.

In the final quadrant, write down five things that you believe you must do before reaching the end of your life.

Happy   Angry

_____   _____
_____   _____
_____   _____
_____   _____
_____   _____
_____

Good At   Must Do

_____   _____
_____   _____
_____   _____
_____   _____
_____   _____

Look carefully at the four quadrants. Can you observe any trends or areas that you identify with?

Truly wealthy people do what they love and love what they do. Once you identify your areas of passion, find a job in that field. Then you'll be on your way to becoming truly wealthy!

Jump out of bed every morning and live with passion!

CHAPTER 4

Avoiding Debt

I've seen more people fail because of liquor and leverage—leverage being borrowed money.

WARREN BUFFETT

THE RISE OF THE CREDIT CARD EMPIRE

We are moving into a cashless world. With the advancement of technology, the use of credit cards has been on the rise in recent years. No doubt this has brought us a lot of conveniences. However, it can be a double-edged sword if we do not know how to watch our spending carefully. Remember these two facts before you use credit cards:

1. Using credit cards incurs very high interest when we do not pay the balance off every month. Warren once said, "Interest rates are very high on credit cards, sometimes they are 18%, sometimes they are 20%. If I borrowed money at 18% or 20%, I'd be broke."
2. Using credit cards encourages us to spend more.

When we spend money using cash, it triggers a sense of loss and makes us hesitate when deciding on purchases. In contrast, cashless transactions, like those using credit cards, dull the pain of paying and make the transactions seem easier. This sense of ease causes people to overspend.

So, how do we prevent ourselves from falling into the credit card trap?

We can follow these two principles.

1. Use cash instead of credit cards. If you are the type of person who does not have the discipline to control their spending, you should adopt a money management system called the "Envelope System." What you do is prepare different envelopes for different expenditure categories. Next, decide the amount you can allocate to each category. For example, you can have an envelope for food, one for transportation, and another for personal shopping. Once you finish spending what you have set aside for each category, it's time to stop.

2. Pay your credit card bills in full, on time. If you still want to enjoy the convenience of credit cards, make sure you do not incur any late fees or interest!

THE DANGER OF DEBT

About ten years ago, a friend of Sean's came to him and asked if he could borrow money. The friend—let's call him Alan—eventually confessed that he could not repay his debt.

Alan told Sean that he had spent too much money using his credit card and did not have enough cash to pay his statement balance. Interest began to kick in, and before Alan knew it, the amount he owed was three times more than his monthly salary.

To "resolve" the matter, Alan naively believed that he could use other credit cards to delay the payment. So he started to apply for many other credit cards and used them to finance his debts. Instead of improving his situation, this made things worse. He had huge debts with five different credit card companies. He was desperate and wanted to obtain some quick cash.

This happened at the time Apple launched the popular iPhone 4. To encourage people to sign up for mobile plans, telecom companies gave away free iPhone 4s to customers who opted for the most expensive mobile plans. Alan saw this as an opportunity and applied for nine mobile lines. He then sold the "free" iPhones to secondhand phone shops. But alas, the amount he got from selling the iPhones was not enough to pay off his debts.

He now owed money to five credit card companies, and in addition, he had to pay for nine telecom lines every month.

Finally, he approached moneylenders. Things got out of hand and the loan sharks started to harass Alan and his family. This is when he called his friends for help.

Sean agreed to help Alan. First, he asked Alan to write down all the money he owed and the respective interest rates for each debt. The two of them then devised a plan in which Alan would pay off one debt at a time, and not charge any more purchases. Eventually, after three years of hard work, Alan managed to clear his debts. Remember: all these troubles stemmed from the overexpenditure of that one credit card!

BORROWING FOR INVESTING

There are people who say that having some debts is good. These people borrow money at a relatively low interest rate and invest it to earn a higher rate of return. In my opinion, the interest from debt is guaranteed, but the return from investments is never guaranteed.

So, unless you are a sophisticated investor who understands how to mitigate risks, and can afford losses, Sean and I encourage you to stay away from borrowing money.

You really don't need leverage. If you're smart, you're going to make a lot of money without borrowing.
WARREN BUFFETT

CHAPTER 5

Risk Management

Warren frequently quotes his two investment rules. Rule number one is to never lose money. Rule number two is to never forget rule number one.

People who try to become wealthy and fail generally fall into two categories. First there are people who take a huge risk in an attempt to get rich quick. They leap before looking and end up crashing at the bottom of the cliff.

Alternatively, there are people who become paralyzed by fear and don't dare to take any risk. They keep their money in the bank, or under their mattress, and let inflation slowly erode their wealth.

Wealthy people are open to investments that can help grow their wealth. They identify risks and mitigate them to the lowest degree possible.

In this chapter, you will learn two risk management actions you can take instantly.

RISK MANAGEMENT ACTION 1:
EMERGENCY FUND

Recently, one of my friends shared on her Facebook page that her heating system was broken and she needed $8,000 to repair it. However, she did not have the money. As we mentioned earlier, not having money for such unforeseen circumstances is dangerous, since we may need to borrow in times of crisis.

On January 6, 2016, Forbes released an article with research from Bankrate.com that 63% of Americans don't have enough savings to cover a $500 emergency. If an emergency occurs, they will have no choice but to borrow money. That is why it is so important to set aside a sum of cash for rainy days.

We recommend you have at least three months' worth of living expenses in liquid savings.

Here are three important principles about your emergency fund.

1. It is not an investment fund.

   This fund is not an investment fund: its existence is not posited on its continuing to grow. Instead, it is meant to be used if you meet an unforeseen financial crisis.

2. It must be accessible.

   The emergency fund should be easily retrievable. For instance, do not put it in real estate, as doing this usually requires a few months before you can access the money by selling a given property.

3. It should be kept out of sight, but not out of reach.

While this emergency fund is accessible, keep it out of sight! It should not be conveniently placed beside your door. If not, you may be tempted to use it to pay for pizza when the deliveryman arrives. My suggestion is to keep it in a separate bank account.

SEAN'S LESSON ON EMERGENCY FUNDS

In January 2009, Sean was shopping with his wife two days before the Chinese New Year. She was pregnant with their second son, and her due date was two months away. Suddenly Sean's wife stopped in her tracks and said, "I think we have to go to the doctor right away."

They rushed to Thomson Medical Center. The next day, their second son was born prematurely.

Sean's wife needed specialized care and had to stay in the hospital longer than originally planned, and as a result, Sean was faced with a huge hospital bill.

At that point in time, he did not have the cash to pay the staggering bill. He was expecting the baby to be delivered two months later, and had planned his finances based on that timeline. Most of his cash was tied up in investments. He had almost no liquid money left to pay the bills.

In the end, he called his very good friend Daniel for help. Fortunately, Daniel lent him a five-figure sum without hesitation. Since that day, Sean has made sure that his family has at least six months' worth of living expenses in their emergency fund!

RISK MANAGEMENT ACTION 2:
AMPLE INSURANCE

Unless you fall into the ultrarich category, you need to make sure you have insurance.

Insurance is a huge topic and it is impossible to cover everything here. That is why Sean and I advise you to enlist the services of a trusted financial adviser to review your needs.

In this section, I will cover the most important aspects of insurance that you should know.

What to Insure?

Our opinion is that at the very least you need insurance to help you manage these two situations:

1. Loss of income
2. Incurring medical expenses

Loss of Income

It is important to make sure that all income earners, and especially people who are the sole breadwinner of the family, have adequate insurance coverage. If you should lose the ability to generate income, the money provided by insurance will help you through the most difficult times.

Although you may think that you are always lucky, life is

unpredictable. One major illness, injury, or accident can easily lead to disability or death. Thus it is better to be safe than sorry. An insurance policy is your safety.

Ask your financial planner if your coverage ensures that either the victim of an accident or the beneficiary of the policy will receive enough cash to tide them over a reasonable period of time should the unfortunate happen.

A good rule of thumb is to have an accident plan and a disability plan, both with coverage for ten years' worth of living expenses.

Let's take Jake as an example. If Jake's yearly expenses are $60,000, it will be good for him to have coverage of $600,000. In other words, if he loses his ability to make a living, his insurance plan should give him or his beneficiary $600,000.

The assumption here is that within ten years, Jake or his family will be able to find a solution to compensate for the loss of income.

Incurring Medical Expenses

If you don't have adequate insurance, medical expenses could wipe out everything that you have accumulated. One might need to sell off investments and businesses, or even take loans to pay for medical bills.

Such cases of unforeseen medical bills can even throw someone who is financially independent into sudden debt.

Our world is one in which people live much longer lives, but also a world in which illnesses and diseases afflict the young as well as the old. That is why we need to continuously review and update our insurance plans to cover as many possible scenarios as possible.

Ask your financial adviser if you are adequately covered should you be involved in an accident or contract a major illness. Also, note that these plans are not limited to breadwinners only.

Everyone in the family should be insured.

Summary Table

The above-mentioned are the important scenarios where we need insurance. Following is a table that summarizes what we have just discussed.

What to cover	Loss of income	Medical expenses
Who to cover	Income earners, especially breadwinners	Everyone in the family
How much to cover	About 10 years of living expenses, or enough to tide the person or the dependents over during the crisis	As much as possible, to fully cover any medical and hospital expenses
When to cover	When one starts to earn income, and more so when one has others depending on his or her income	Right now!

CHAPTER 6

Taking Care of Your Health

Warren once shared this story about a genie.

"When I was sixteen, I had just two things on my mind—girls and cars. I wasn't very good with girls. So I thought about cars. I thought about girls, too, but I had more luck with cars.

"Let's say that when I turned sixteen, a genie had appeared to me. And that genie said, 'Warren, I'm going to give you the car of your choice. It'll be here tomorrow morning with a big bow tied around it. Brand-new. And it's all yours.'

"Having heard all the genie stories, I would say, 'What's the catch?' And the genie would answer, 'There's only one catch. This is the last car you're ever going to get in your life. So it's got to last a lifetime.'

"If that had happened, I would have picked out that car. But, can you imagine, knowing it had to last a lifetime, what I would do with it?

"I would read the manual about five times. I would always keep it garaged. If there was the least little dent or scratch, I'd have it fixed right away, because if anything went wrong, I wouldn't want the car to be rusting. I would baby that car, because it would have to last a lifetime.

"That's exactly how I look at people. We have one mind

and one body, and they have to last a lifetime. If you don't take care of your mind and body, they'll be a wreck, just like a car might be. What you do today determines how your mind and body will operate 10, 20, and 30 years from now."

OUR GREATEST ASSETS

As Warren noted, our body and our mind are the biggest assets we have. You may have heard about Warren's eating habits and question this . . .

Warren once said his secret to staying young was to "eat like a six-year-old." This includes drinking up to five cans of Coke a day, and eating hamburgers, steaks, and sundaes for breakfast. But Warren takes care of himself.

In 2007 (at the age of 77), Warren revealed that his doctor had asked him to make a simple choice—either eat better or exercise. Warren chose the latter, believing that it was, as he put it, "the lesser of two evils."

We will not go in depth on how to stay healthy because there is plenty of information out there. The key is to build habits that keep us healthy. And we all know the two simple facts: eat better and exercise!

Set aside some time each week to exercise and observe how your body responds. Sean exercises every day and Mary is careful about what she eats. You will be surprised how youthful you can become!

CHAPTER 7

Continuous Improvement

Warren Buffett has become one hell of a lot better investor since the day I met him, and so have I. If we had been frozen at any given stage, with the knowledge we had, the record would have been much worse than it is. So the game is to keep learning.

CHARLIE MUNGER

Truly wealthy people never stop learning and improving. Besides upgrading your technical skills, here are some suggestions I would like you to consider implementing in your life.

INNER SCORECARD

Warren has what he calls an inner scorecard. He asks, "Would you rather be the world's greatest lover, but have everyone think you're the world's worst lover? Or would you like to be the world's worst lover but have everyone think you're the world's greatest lover?"

Now, that's an interesting question.

If all the emphasis is on what the world's going to think about you, not about how you really behave, you'll wind up with an *outer scorecard*.

There are people who strive to win recognition, and they lose themselves in the process. What really matters is who *you* become in the process.

INTEGRITY, INTELLIGENCE, ENERGY

Speaking to a group of MBA students, Warren said, "I would like to talk about your future. You will learn a tremendous amount about investments in this MBA program; you all have the ability to do well; you all have the intelligence to do well. You all have the energy and initiative to do well or you wouldn't be here.

"But in determining whether you succeed there is more to consider than intellect and energy.

"There was a guy, Pete Kiewit, in Omaha, who used to say he looked for three things when he hired people: integrity, intelligence, and energy. And he said if the person did not have the first, the latter two would kill him, because if they don't have integrity, you want them dumb and lazy.

"What if I granted you the right to buy 10% of one of your classmate's earnings for the rest of their lifetime? You can't choose someone with family money; you have to pick someone who is going to succeed on his or her own merit. Will you give them an IQ test and pick the one with the highest IQ? I doubt it.

"Will you pick the one with the best grades? The most energetic? You will probably start looking for qualitative factors, in addition [to the quantitative] because everyone has enough brains and energy.

"You would likely pick the person you responded to best, the one who has the leadership qualities, is generous, honest, and who gave credit to other people for their ideas.

"You wouldn't pick the person with the lowest IQ, you wouldn't think about the person who turned you off, the person who is egotistical, who is greedy, who cuts corners, who is slightly dishonest.

"You'll see positive qualities that you can cultivate, and negative qualities that you can shy away from.

"You can get rid of negative behaviors. You can get rid of them a lot easier at your age than at my age, because most behaviors are habitual. Warren says the chains of habit are too light to be felt until you try to break them. There is no question about it. I see people with self-destructive behavior patterns at my age and even twenty years younger entrapped by their negativity.

"Their actions and attitudes constantly turn off people. They don't need to be difficult or dishonest but they don't know how to change lifelong bad habits."

But at your age you can develop any habits, any patterns of behavior that you wish. It is simply a question of what you decide you want.

Warren noticed that many successful people look for people whom they want to emulate. When Benjamin Graham— one of Warren's teachers—was a young teenager, he looked around at the people he admired and he decided, "I want to be admired, so why don't I behave like them?"

Warren continued, "Graham discovered that there was nothing impossible about behaving like people he admired.

I would suggest that if you write down the positive qualities you admire in others and think about them awhile, and make them habitual, you will be the person whose earnings you want to buy 10% of. And the beauty of this is that you already own 100% of these assets. So you might as well be the best person possible."

THE QUALITIES EXERCISE

Take a moment to think about what Warren told the MBA students. Think of the people you admire and respect. Following, in the left-hand column, write down the qualities you admire in these people.

Then take some time to think about people you detest. And write down the qualities you associate with these people in the right-hand column.

Look at your chart . . .

Qualities You Admire	Qualities You Detest
_____	_____
_____	_____
_____	_____
_____	_____
_____	_____
_____	_____
_____	_____
_____	_____
_____	_____

Have you identified the areas you want to work on? Strive to work on them a little every day. As Charlie Munger said, "Spend each day trying to be wiser than you were when you woke up."

SECRET 2

THE POWER OF
VALUE INVESTING

What Is Value Investing?

Do you know someone who has a huge collection of stamps? Or someone who loves to collect baseball cards?

Imagine instead of stamps or cards, what you have is a collection of the most profitable businesses in the world.

This is what investing is about.

Warren has some of the most profitable businesses such as Coca-Cola, Kraft Foods, and American Express in his investment portfolio.

Pause for a moment and imagine: each time someone buys a soft drink from Coca-Cola, a snack from Kraft Foods, or uses a card from American Express, you become richer!

Just a quick fact: about 1.9 billion Coca-Colas are sold in a single day.

That is 79 million cans of Coke every hour, which is equivalent to 1.3 million cans per minute, 21,990 cans per second.

1 second, 2 seconds, 3 seconds . . .

That is about 65,000 cans of Coke sold. And if you own "The Coca-Cola Company," you will be 65,000 cans of Coke richer every three seconds.

That is the idea of investing! To buy and own profitable businesses!

And in the stock market, you can own these businesses by buying their shares.

What about value?

Value stands for buying a good business at a good price. You may be wondering why some people who have bought shares of profitable businesses do not make money from the stock market. The explanation is simple: they bought it at an overvalued price.

That is why it is so crucial to learn value investing, which advocates buying good and profitable businesses at sensible prices. And by practicing value investing you will gradually master the secret to building lasting wealth.

CHAPTER 9

Origins of Value Investing

Mary and I want to acknowledge the origins of value investing as we induct you into the value investing community. To understand value investing and how it has impacted lives, let's go back to the first half of the twentieth century. In 1934, two finance professors from Columbia Business School, Benjamin Graham and David Dodd, published a book called *Security Analysis*, which became *the* guidebook for successful brokers and investors.

Before *Security Analysis* was published, people who invested in the stock market were guided largely by speculation and what they believed to be insider information. (It doesn't seem much different from today, does it?)

Benjamin Graham believed that by studying and analyzing the market, he would be able to determine a stock's "real" price; then, when he purchased it, he would be doing so as a knowledgeable professional rather than a mere speculator. He worked with David Dodd to develop value investing—a strategy that is used to identify and buy stocks below their value, or *undervalue*.

Graham began teaching the method of value investing at Columbia Business School in 1928 and continued to improve his skills over time. Some of the legendary businessmen who attended his class were Warren Buffett ('51), Mario Gabelli ('67), Glenn Greenberg ('73), Charles Royce ('63), Walter Schloss ('78), and John Shapiro ('78). In the next chapters, we will discuss some of these great investors and how we can learn from them.

In 1992, Tweedy, Browne Company LLC published *What Has Worked in Investing—Studies of Investment Approaches and Characteristics Associated with Exceptional Results.* The company's analysts examined the concept of "value" in different markets and in various scenarios over time and concluded that value investing always produced remarkable returns.

Each of us has only a few decades in which to invest, so we need to follow a proven method in order to make our money grow. The rest of this book will explain how to use value investing to make your own money grow.

Welcome to the value investing community.

GENERATING

STOCKS IDEAS

CHAPTER 10

How Do We Start Finding Stock Investments?

FINDING STOCKS LOGICALLY

When I first met Mary, I asked her the following question.

"So where do we start to find great stocks we can invest in?"

She replied with a question of her own. "What characteristics do you think we look for in great stocks?"

"Well," I answered, "if I'm looking for great stocks, I want them to possess these qualities:

1. _____

2. _____

3. _____

4. _____

5. _____

"These are the characteristics I will look for," I concluded.

Now pause for a moment before you fill in the blanks above. Remember to think in terms of businesses. If you were to invest in a business, what kind of business do you want to invest in?

What characteristics would you look for?

Now write down at least five characteristics before we compare notes.

This is an extremely important exercise in your path to success in value investing. In subsequent chapters, we will go through some of the key criteria we should look at, but for now, try to come up with some ideas of your own so that you can assess your mind-set as a business investor.

Have you written at least five characteristics? If so, great job!

Now let's continue our conversation with Mary.

"Well, if I'm looking for great stocks, I want them to possess these qualities:

1. Profitable business
2. Lots of loyal customers
3. Always ahead of trends
4. Market leader
5. Good growth potential

"These are the characteristics I will look for," I answered.

"That's right!" Mary responded. "And where do you think we can find great stocks that possess these characteristics?" she asked.

"Well," I said, "some possible places will be . . .

1. _____
2. _____
3. _____
4. _____
5. _____"

Okay now! It's thinking time again. This is a book that gives you answers. We want to help you become a good investor and think for yourself. Given the characteristics we have stated above, where do you think we could logically find businesses that possess them?

Go ahead; use your imagination and fill in the preceding blanks with five ideas.

Here are some possible answers:

1. Visit shopping malls to see which shops have a lot of customers.
2. Observe what items you have to buy on a regular basis and determine which companies you will buy them from.
3. Google the companies with top-rated brands.
4. Check out what seasoned investors are investing in.
5. Use investment screeners.

Mary exclaimed with joy, "Yeah! These are wonderful ideas. We do that all the time."

"Really? You guys do that?" I asked.

"Yes, we do. Why not? It's logical, isn't it?"

In the following chapters, we will explore several ways to find stock ideas that we can use to build our portfolio.

Note that while your list of ideas may not be exhaustive—certainly ours is not either—some of them may turn out to be quite ingenious.

One of your suggestions could turn out to put you in touch with your own special edge as an investor. If this is the case, I hope you'll share it with me so that I can add it to my own arsenal of weapons.

CHAPTER 11

Circle of Competence

The first important step an investor must take is to determine where to invest. Warren calls this the circle of competence.

Here is an excerpt from his 1996 letter to Berkshire Hathaway shareholders:

> *Should you choose . . . to construct your own portfolio, there are a few thoughts worth remembering. Intelligent investing is not complex, though that is far from saying that it is easy. What an investor needs is the ability to correctly evaluate selected businesses. Note that word "selected": You don't have to be an expert on every company, or even many. You only have to be able to evaluate companies within your circle of competence. The size of that circle is not very important; knowing its boundaries, however, is vital.*

You may find this to be somewhat limited in focus, but I would like you to remember that as an investor, you are buying businesses. Therefore, it is important that you buy what you understand and what you are interested in.

Since you are spending money on, or earning money from,

a business, you will need to have some idea of how that business works.

Warren Buffett avoids businesses that are outside his circle of competence. He once said, "If we can't find things within our circle of competence, we don't expand the circle. We'll wait."

This is not to say that we should not learn about businesses we do not understand. Rather, it is a warning not to rush into something we do not understand just because the businesses we understand are not selling at a sensible price.

FINDING BUSINESSES IN YOUR CIRCLE OF COMPETENCE

Let's start by finding some businesses you have some understanding of. Start with the following exercise:

List the names of businesses you earn your money from. (These can be your company and your company's clients.)

_____

_____

_____

_____

List the names of businesses where you spend your money. (If you have been keeping track of your credit card bills or your bank GIRO payments, pull them out and see where your money has been going to month after month. These businesses have at least one loyal customer—YOU!)

_____

_____

_____

_____

_____

Now list some of your areas of expertise. These can be your talents—e.g., exercise, singing, cooking, computer programming, investing, teaching.

_____

_____

_____

_____

_____

Lastly, list some things you have an interest in and passion for. These can be your hobbies, or a particular subject that you would like to learn more about.

_____

_____

_____

_____

_____

When you have written this list, you may find an intersection between the things you spend money on, make money from, and have talent in and a passion for. It might look something like this:

_____

_____

_____

_____

_____

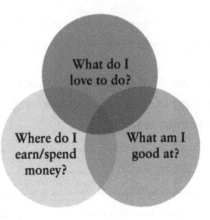

This is a possible example:

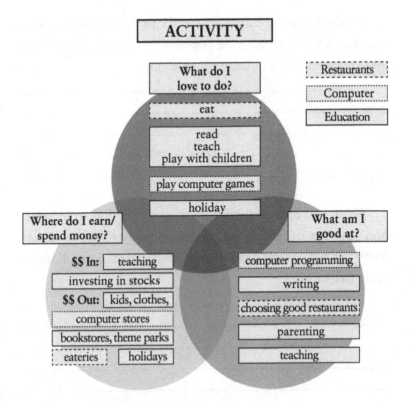

Here is a blank diagram for you to fill in to find your own sweet spot. If you are feeling a little stuck, we have included a list of sectors and industries for you to look through to give you some ideas.

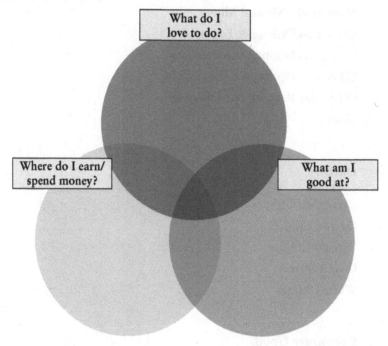

Here are some possible sectors and industries. You can circle those that are familiar to you and focus on them.

Basic Materials

Agricultural Chemicals
Aluminum
Chemicals—Major Diversified
Copper

Gold
Independent Oil & Gas
Industrial Metals & Minerals
Major Integrated Oil & Gas
Nonmetallic Mineral Mining
Oil & Gas Drilling & Exploration
Oil & Gas Equipment & Services
Oil & Gas Pipelines
Oil & Gas Refining & Marketing
Silver

Utilities

Diversified Utilities
Electric Utilities
Foreign Utilities
Gas Utilities
Water Utilities

Consumer Goods

Beverages—Wineries & Distillers
Business Equipment
Cigarettes
Cleaning Products
Confectioners
Dairy Products
Electronic Equipment
Farm Products
Food—Major Diversified

Home Furnishings & Fixtures
Housewares & Accessories
Meat Products
Office Supplies
Packaging & Containers
Paper & Paper Products
Personal Products
Photographic Equipment & Supplies
Processed & Packaged Goods
Recreational Goods
Recreational Vehicles
Rubber & Plastics
Sporting Goods
Textile—Apparel Clothing
Textile—Apparel Footwear & Accessories
Tobacco Products
Toys & Games
Trucks & Other Vehicles

Health Care

Biotechnology
Diagnostic Substances
Drug Delivery
Drug Manufacturers—Major
Drug Manufacturers—Other
Drug-Related Products
Drugs—Generic
Health Care Plans
Home Health Care

Hospitals
Long-Term Care Facilities
Medical Appliances & Equipment
Medical Instruments & Supplies
Medical Laboratories & Research
Medical Practitioners
Specialized Health Services

Financial

Accident & Health Insurance
Asset Management
Closed-End Fund—Debt
Closed-End Fund—Equity
Closed-End Fund—Foreign
Credit Services
Diversified Investments
Foreign Money Center Banks
Foreign Regional Banks
Investment Brokerage—Regional
Life Insurance
Money Center Banks
Mortgage Investment
Property & Casualty Insurance
Property Management
Real Estate Development
REIT (Real Estate Investment Trust)—Diversified
REIT—Health Care Facilities
REIT—Hotel/Motel
REIT—Industrial

REIT—Office

REIT—Residential

REIT—Retail

Regional—Mid-Atlantic Banks

Regional—Midwest Banks

Regional—Northeast Banks

Regional—Pacific Banks

Regional—Southeast Banks

Regional—Southwest Banks

Savings & Loans

Surety & Title Insurance

Industrial Goods

Aerospace/Defense—Major Diversified

Aerospace/Defense Products & Services

Cement

Diversified Machinery

Farm & Construction Machinery

General Building Materials

General Contractors

Heavy Construction

Industrial Electrical Equipment

Industrial Equipment & Components

Lumber, Wood Production

Machine Tools & Accessories

Manufactured Housing

Metal Fabrication

Pollution & Treatment Controls

Residential Construction

Small Tools & Accessories

Textile Industrial

Waste Management

Technology

Application Software

Business Software & Services

Communication Equipment

Computer Peripherals

Data Storage Devices

Diversified Communication Services

Diversified Computer Systems

Diversified Electronics

Health Care Information Services

Information & Delivery Services

Information Technology Services

Internet Information Providers

Internet Service Providers

Internet Software & Services

Long-Distance Carriers

Multimedia & Graphics Software

Networking & Communication Devices

Personal Computers

Printed Circuit Boards

Processing Systems & Products

Scientific & Technical Instruments

Security Software & Services

Semiconductor—Broad Line

Semiconductor—Equipment & Materials

Semiconductor—Integrated Circuits
Semiconductor—Specialized
Technical & System Software
Telecom Services—Domestic
Telecom Services—Foreign
Wireless Communications

Services

Advertising Agencies
Air Delivery & Freight Services
Air Services
Apparel Stores
Auto Dealerships
Auto Parts Stores
Auto Parts Wholesale
Basic Materials Wholesale
Broadcasting—Radio
Broadcasting—TV
Building Materials Wholesale
Business Services
Catalog & Mail-Order Houses
CATV Systems
Computers Wholesale
Consumer Services
Department Stores
Discount, Variety Stores
Drugs Wholesale
Drugstores
Education & Training Services

Electronics Stores
Electronics Wholesale
Entertainment—Diversified
Food Wholesale
Gaming Activities
General Entertainment
Grocery Stores
Home Improvement Stores
Industrial Equipment Wholesale
Jewelry Stores
Lodging
Management Services
Marketing Services
Medical Equipment Wholesale
Movie Production, Theaters
Music & Video Stores
Personal Services
Publishing—Books
Publishing—Newspapers
Publishing—Periodicals
Railroads
Regional Airlines
Rental & Leasing Services
Research Services
Resorts & Casinos
Restaurants
Security & Protection Services
Shipping
Specialty Eateries
Specialty Retail

Sporting Activities
Sporting Goods Stores
Staffing & Outsourcing Services
Technical Services
Toy & Hobby Stores
Trucking

Conclusion

It is really important to know which areas you should look into before you begin investing. If we try to be good at everything, it is likely that we will end up being mediocre at many things.

So write down at least three areas or segments that you think you have a true interest in. In the next few chapters, we will look into ways to hunt for stock ideas that match our circle of competence.

CHAPTER 12

Financial Websites

As Mary and I are writing this chapter, we are sure that new financial websites are being created and suspect that these may be the websites that we will be using next as we research possible investments.

As of now, however, the following list contains the names of websites that we are currently using to find stock ideas.

Bookmark these and get constant updates.

1. Yahoo! Finance (http://finance.yahoo.com/)

Based on our observations, Yahoo! Finance publishes finance news really quickly. Whenever you have time, go to this site to read about news currently in the spotlight. We will be interested . . . well, cough, cough . . . what we'll be interested in actually is bad news.

The reason for this is that when a company has bad news, its stock price will most likely fall because people will tend to overreact. We want to find companies that have gotten into some temporary trouble that will not affect their business models dramatically, and to buy shares in these companies when they become undervalued.

2. Seeking Alpha (https://seekingalpha.com/)

Seeking Alpha is a platform that allows contributors from all over the world to share their opinions on stock investments.

Many investment enthusiasts contribute their insights on a daily basis, and you can easily find information here that you cannot get elsewhere. Seeking Alpha is a great place to source for investment ideas.

However, you need to differentiate opinions from facts because opinions tend to be highly subjective.

3. Buffett Online School (https://www.facebook.com/buffettonlineschoolglobal/)

This is our Facebook page and we constantly share carefully crafted investment videos and articles in order to educate the public on value investing.

The information is suitable for new investors. Follow us and pose any questions you may have on investing.

Our investment analysts will answer you on a weekly basis.

4. MarketWatch (www.marketwatch.com)

Another website that has regularly updated news is MarketWatch.

It also provides a virtual stock exchange so that you can have ample practice before diving into the real market. One note: MarketWatch is very U.S.-centric.

5. *The Wall Street Journal* (www.wsj.com/)

This website provides financial information on stocks all over the world. Search for individual stocks in the search box, and you will be provided with four years of financial data moments later.

6. GuruFocus (www.gurufocus.com)

This website tracks the investment portfolio of some of the most famous investors in the world. It has a lot of insightful articles that relate to value investing as well.

7. The Motley Fool (www.fool.com)

The Motley Fool is a stock advisory website that provides opinions beyond financial data, including useful information about business potential and company culture.

These websites will come in handy once you finish reading this book and start to assess and evaluate companies as possible investments.

CHAPTER 13

Tracking the Richest Man

Have you ever thought about how the richest people on Earth build their wealth? Many of them are either entrepreneurs or investors. For example, Jeff Bezos made it to the top of the *Forbes* list of richest people through holding shares of Amazon and Mark Zuckerberg through shares of Facebook. Wouldn't it be nice if we could get some of these brilliant businessmen to build our wealth?

The interesting thing is that many of them have kindly listed their companies on the stock exchanges and we can invest into their companies and tap into their ability to create wealth. This is one of the ways we go hunting for good stock-investing ideas.

By googling *"Forbes* Richest," we will be able to see the latest list of the wealthiest people on earth and read about how they make their wealth. We are likely to regularly see some of these names and their sources of wealth on the list.

1. Bill Gates (Microsoft)
2. Warren Buffett (Berkshire Hathaway)
3. Larry Page (Google)
4. Larry Ellison (Oracle)
5. The Walton family (Walmart)

If you noticed, most of the companies are available for us to invest in through the stock market. So go ahead and do your own search for the latest list. Go through the list and you will find many investing ideas.

CHAPTER 14

Best Companies

In the previous chapter, we shared that one of the ways to get investment ideas is to search for the list of wealthiest people and their sources of wealth. Another way is to look at companies that have good working culture.

After all, great companies are made great by the people who work in them. Hence, it is a good idea to invest in companies where the employees are happy.

To get a list of such companies, we can visit Fortune or Glassdoor. These sites will rank companies based on employee satisfaction on an annual basis. Based on our search on May 22, 2019, some companies that are ranked in the top 100 for both Fortune "Best Companies to Work For" and Glassdoor's "Best Places to Work: Employees' Choice" include

1. Salesforce (Ranked 11 in Glassdoor and 2 in Fortune)
2. Cisco (Ranked 69 in Glassdoor and 6 in Fortune)
3. Intuit (Ranked 38 in Glassdoor and 24 in Fortune)

These are good places to list companies that we may want to do more research on. So go ahead and open your web browser and start your search for the latest list. You may be pleasantly surprised at what you may find.

CHAPTER 15

Shopping Mall

Warren Buffett is known to have said that he prefers look-ing for stocks on Main Street rather than Wall Street. Some of his top holdings include Kraft, Coca-Cola, American Express, and Wells Fargo & Company. Guess how he found these stock ideas.

The answer: *He is a customer of these businesses.*

In chapter 5, we discussed the notion of the circle of com-petence and how to find businesses to invest in. If you enjoy shopping, you can easily find some good companies just like Warren did.

Even if you don't love shopping, you can still identify good businesses by paying more attention to the following:

1. Which shops have a lot of customers and have been in existence for many years?

   _____

   _____

   _____

   _____

   _____

   _____

   _____

2. Which products and services are popular and growing?

_____
_____
_____
_____
_____
_____
_____
_____

3. What necessities do many people buy on a regularly recurring basis?

_____
_____
_____
_____
_____
_____
_____

4. What products must supermarkets carry?

_____
_____
_____
_____
_____
_____
_____

5. What products must big retail stores carry?

_____

_____

_____

_____

_____

_____

_____

If you look at the five lists you've made, you might find some of the companies you want to invest in. If so, go to the financial websites we discussed in chapter 12 and look at the business to see if they have the kind of qualities that would make you want to invest in them.

CHAPTER 16

Best Value Investors

In this chapter, you are going to learn one of the most direct and useful ways to find stock ideas: look at the portfolios of the best value investors in the world. At this point, it is important to track only value investors. The reason for this is that unlike short-term traders, who buy and sell on a regular basis, value investors hold on to their portfolios for years.

Moreover, trying to track short-term traders is useless because their portfolios change too quickly and dramatically to yield any significant research information.

In this chapter, we are going to introduce you to some of the best value investors you can follow. To search for their portfolios, just Google "investor name + portfolio."

Following is a list of some of the greatest investors in the world.

1. Warren Buffett

Warren Buffett is the chairman and CEO of Berkshire Hathaway. As of March 2019, the top five largest stock holdings in his portfolio are:

S/No	Ticker	Company	Industry
1	AAPL	Apple Inc.	Consumer Electronics
2	BAC	Bank of America	Banks
3	WFC	Wells Fargo & Co.	Banks
4	KO	Coca-Cola Co.	Beverages—Nonalcoholic
5	AXP	American Express Co.	Credit Services

2. Howard Marks

Howard Marks helped to fund Oaktree Capital Management in 1995. Before that, he served as the chief investment officer for domestic fixed income at the TCW Group, Inc., overseeing distressed debt, high-yield bonds, and convertible securities investments.

As of March 2019, the top-five highest weighted stocks in his portfolio are:

S/No	Ticker	Company	Industry
1	VST	Vistra Energy Corp.	Utilities
2	TRMD	Torm PLC	Industrials
3	SBLK	Star Bulk Carriers Corp.	Transportation and Logistics
4	ALLY	Ally Financial Inc.	Banks
5	TSM	Taiwan Semiconductor	Semiconductor

3. Joel Greenblatt

Joel Greenblatt runs Gotham Asset Management with his partner Robert Goldstein. He is an adjunct professor at Columbia University and is the author of two very good books, *The Little Book That Beats the Market* and *You Can Be a Stock Market Genius.*

He is an investing legend who has been using a strategy that he called the Magic Formula to generate 30%-plus annualized returns after launching Gotham in 1985.

As of March 2019, the top-five highest weighted stocks in his portfolio are:

S/No	Ticker	Company	Industry
1	HON	Honeywell International Inc.	Diversified Industrials
2	VZ	Verizon Communications Inc.	Telecom Services
3	AAPL	Apple Inc.	Consumer Electronics
4	MO	Altria Group Inc.	Tobacco
5	PYPL	PayPal Holdings Inc.	Credit Services

4. Seth Klarman

Seth Klarman is an iconic hedge fund manager and expert in value investing.

As of March 2019, the top-five highest weighted stocks in his portfolio are:

S/No	Ticker	Company	Industry
1	FOXA	Twenty-First Century Fox Inc.	Entertainment
2	LNG	Cheniere Energy Inc.	Oil & Gas—Midstream
3	VSAT	Viasat Inc.	Communication Equipment
4	QRVO	Qorvo Inc.	Semiconductors
5	AGN	Allergan PLC	Drug Manufacturers—Specialty & Generic

5. Mario Gabelli

Mario Gabelli has been managing GAMCO Investors since its inception in 1986. He was named Morningstar's Fund Manager of the Year in 1997 and the Institutional Investor's Money Manager of the Year in 2010.

As of March 2019, the top-five largest stock holdings in his portfolio are:

S/No	Ticker	Company	Industry
1	MSG	The Madison Square Garden Co.	Leisure
2	SNE	Sony Corp.	Consumer Electronics
3	BK	Bank of New York Mellon Corp.	Asset Management
4	RHP	Ryman Hospitality Properties Inc.	REIT—Hotel & Motel
5	FOX	Twenty-First Century Fox Inc.	Entertainment

6. Glenn Greenberg

Glenn Greenberg was the cofounder of Chief-tain Capital with John Shapiro in 1984. In late 2009 the duo parted ways due to personal con-flicts and Greenberg remained at the existing firm, renaming it Brave Warrior Advisors.

As of March 2019, the top-five highest weighted stocks in his portfolio are:

S/No	Ticker	Company	Industry
1	GOOGL	Alphabet Inc.	Internet content & information
2	ADS	Alliance Data Systems Corp.	Credit services
3	SCHW	Charles Schwab Corp.	Capital markets
4	JPM	JPMorgan Chase & Co.	Banks
5	RJF	Raymond James Financial Inc.	Capital markets

7. Thomas S. Gayner

Thomas S. Gayner has been the head of Markel Gayner Asset Management (Markel's investment division) since 1990. Markel has been called the mini Berkshire Hathaway.

As of writing in March 2019, the top-five high-est weighted stocks in his portfolio are:

S/No	Ticker	Company	Industry
1	BRK.A	Berkshire Hathaway Inc.	Insurance
2	KMX	CarMax Inc.	Autos
3	BAM	Brookfield Asset Management Inc.	Real estate services
4	DIS	Walt Disney Co.	Entertainment
5	DEO	Diageo PLC	Beverages— wineries & distilleries

CONCLUSION

We can literally find information regarding what the best value investors in the world are doing and gain ideas from their actions. It is almost as if these best value investors work for us to help us build our portfolios. Our website also constantly tracks the latest movements and actions of these best value investors: www.buffettonlineschool.com.

SECRET 4

ECONOMIC MOATS

CHAPTER 17

What Is an Economic Moat?

Prior to becoming a full-time investor, I was a military officer. Upon reflection, there were many military strategies that are parallel and can be used in investing.

When I was a trainee in the officer school, I learned an important lesson that I use in investing. We were doing a two-sided military exercise in which we were supposed to hunt down and eliminate the other team using simulated laser weapons. This was our first mission, and it was led by our team leader, Alfred. We were all pumped up. (Note that all our conversations were in whispers, as we were hiding from our enemies.)

"Great! Let's take them down! Come on, let's go!" Alfred commanded confidently.

We put our weapons on ready and began to move when our officer held up his palm to signal a halt.

"Where do you think you guys are going?" he asked.

"To eliminate the other team, sir!" Alfred answered without hesitation.

"And how are you going to eliminate them?" our officer continued to question.

"Er . . . by shooting at them?" Alfred, like the rest of us, was obviously confused by the officer's question.

"If you guys go out there now, there is only a 50% chance you can actually eliminate them. And on top of that, even if your team wins, a lot of you will end up dead," our officer firmly explained.

We were becoming more confused by the moment. After all, isn't getting injured or killed part and parcel of what fighting is about?

"Can you guys tell me what makes you so sure you can defeat the other team? How many troops do you guys have and how many do they have?" our officer asked.

"We have seven in our team and they have seven as well, sir!" Alfred answered.

"So you guys are going out there to fight without any advantage?" Our officer sounded bewildered.

"Sir, we are stronger and faster!" one of our section members, Edwin, voiced his opinion.

"And that's what they'll think, too," our officer replied.

Seeing that we were confused, he signaled for us to sit down and explained, "In warfare, we cannot go into a fight without being highly confident of winning. It would be tantamount to sending our troops on a possible suicide mission.

"Whenever we are fighting enemies, we want to make sure we have more troops, at least three times the number of our enemy's troops, before fighting any other unit. This will give us an obvious advantage and significantly increase our chances of winning. Do you guys understand?"

"Yes, sir!" we replied.

"But in this case, there are seven guys on each side, so there is no way we can have an obvious advantage," I said.

"Besides having more troops, what are other ways we

can gain an advantage over the other team? Use your brains before you start running into the open and getting yourself killed," our officer challenged.

We began to brainstorm and ideas started to flow as we recalled the lectures of our officers back in the lecture theater.

"What have you guys thought of so far?" our officer asked after a while.

"Sir, one way of gaining an advantage is by using terrain," Firdaus, another team member, replied. "We can fight them on the top of a hill and pin them down. It's much more difficult to fight uphill, and from the top of the hill, we will be able to see them much better than they can see us."

"Excellent example of gaining an advantage!" our officer exclaimed. "Unfortunately, as you can see, the next hill is more than three kilometers away and it will be difficult to draw the enemy there. But good thinking, nonetheless." Our officer nodded in acknowledgment. "Any other ideas?"

"Sir, another way is to call for artillery fire on them before we engage. In this way, they will already be injured and some of them might even have been killed. We will then have a greater advantage," Kevin said.

"Good! However, we do not have artillery supporting us in fighting a section. Keep the ideas coming in!" Our officer looked pleased.

After some discussion, we decided to spring an ambush on the other team. (Note that this entire conversation took less than five minutes . . . I don't want you to think we had an hour of discussion.)

"If we can successfully ambush them by hiding around the bend we predict they will be moving along, we can not only gain an advantage by surprising them but can also have better cover in whatever fight ensues." Alfred presented our plans to our officer.

Even with his camouflaged face, our officer could not conceal his smile. He gave us a thumbs up and we launched our action. We quietly moved to the location, where we hid ourselves and waited for the enemy to approach. After waiting 15 minutes, they walked right into our designated target area.

"Fire!" Alfred yelled, and we mercilessly fired rounds of bullets at our enemies. Before any of them could react or locate our place of concealment, we successfully wiped out the entire section without any of our teammates being injured or killed, except Alfred, who suffered a sore throat from yelling all the fighting commands.

The key lesson we took away that day was to always have an advantage in a fight.

The Economic Moat:
An Advantage in the Business World

We often apply the strategy of finding an advantage in the investment world. We try to invest only in businesses that have an advantage over their competitors. Warren Buffett likes to explain this advantage metaphorically, using the analogy of a moat around a castle to ensure you have extra protection.

He calls this an Economic Moat.

Imagine that a business is like a castle. One of the ways the castle can survive attacks is to have a moat around it. The deeper and wider the moat, the less vulnerable the castle will be when it's attacked.

A castle surrounded by a moat is akin to a business that has a durable competitive advantage that makes it possible for the business to consistently attract and retain customers.

This allows the business to make exceptional profits when times are good and continue to do so and survive even when times are bad. Having the moat allows it to raise its prices and retain its customers.

Businesses without an Economic Moat will find themselves struggling during difficult times. Some of them end up bankrupt as a result.

When the economy improves, businesses with Economic Moats enjoy even greater profits because many of their rivals have been wiped out.

Identifying Moats

To find out if a business has a durable competitive advantage, answer these five questions:

The Five Questions

1. What is the value (products/services) this business is providing?
2. Is this value provided by anyone else?
3. Will I choose to get this value from this business or someone else?

4. Why would I rather get this value from this business instead of others?
5. Is the reason(s) you identified in question four sustainable in the long run?

In the following chapters, we will be looking at different types of Economic Moats in order to differentiate strong businesses from weak ones.

CHAPTER 18

Branding

What brands immediately come to your mind when the following products are mentioned?

Soft Drinks
Diapers
Baby Care Products
Fast Food
Furniture
Newspapers

I regularly spend my money on these items; they form my circle of competence. Most people think of either Coke or Pepsi when it comes to soft drinks, Pampers when diapers are mentioned, and Johnson & Johnson for baby care products. In fact, Pampers' branding is so strong that when we run out of diapers, we often say that we need to go and get more Pampers instead of diapers. These businesses have trained us into immediately associating a specific product with a brand.

The first brand most people think of when they need to buy furniture is IKEA. Note that I say *most* people, because there will always be consumers who do not favor the above-mentioned brands. Even so, it is difficult not to think of these brands in relation to a given product. These companies have built their brands so strongly that they own a piece of your mind.

Businesses with strong brands are likely to possess a durable competitive advantage.

Some businesses are able to differentiate their products and services from their competitors in a striking way. Even though they are competing in a particular industry, their products and services have a way of standing out from the crowd.

A good example is the iPhone. The iPhone is not just any phone. It has characteristics and qualities that people want to associate themselves with. It is more than just a phone.

Another example is Kentucky Fried Chicken. When you want to eat fried chicken, KFC stands out as the brand that drives hungry customers into the stores.

However, having a strong brand is not enough to ensure a durable competitive advantage. The brand must translate to profits. Even if *Pampers* or *Kodak* comes to the top of your mind when we talk about diapers or cameras, we may not buy that particular brand. One way to check whether a brand has a competitive advantage is to ask if the business is able to price its products higher than its competitors.

Let's look at Nike. The company's superior brand identity allows it to price products higher than its competitors and still attract customers. Are you aware that Burger King and McDonald's burgers cost much more than burgers without any branding?

THE COMPLEXITY OF A
HIGH-INNOVATION NEED INDUSTRY

We need to be able to identify businesses that can protect their product's differentiation either through branding or legal means. So product differentiation is a good place to start when you're looking for businesses to invest in. In our high-tech world, the uniqueness of a product can be quickly compromised when competitors model their versions of the product after leading brands.

If we find that a business that we are looking to buy into has to constantly innovate to survive, we need to be careful. These businesses may not have a strong moat.

What we want to look for are businesses with products and services that do not require too much research and development. This doesn't mean that businesses shouldn't invest heavily in R&D, but we want to avoid businesses that *require* R&D in order to survive.

Let's revisit the example of the iPhone and KFC. Even though the iPhone is a unique and outstanding product at this point in time, we need to note that industry leaders can change quickly when more innovative products are developed.

Samsung, for example, is a market leader that is in competition with the iPhone. Although the iPhone has many loyal customers, most people will be ready to jump ship to try out another company's phone that offers new, innovative features.

KFC, on the other hand, requires little or no innovation to survive. Colonel Sanders's finger-lickin' recipe remains unchanged, despite the development of the new products that have been introduced from time to time—different-flavored chicken, cheesy fries, Banditos, and salads, for example. Some new products stayed on the menu due to popularity, while others were short-lived.

But the products we're talking about here are add-ons that help the company increase profits rather than determining the survivability of the company. Most of KFC's customers come for the 100-plus-year-old finger-lickin'-good fried chicken. KFC has a more durable competitive advantage in terms of product innovation than the iPhone.

CHAPTER 19

Economy of Scale

Some businesses are so huge and so efficient that they can undercut their competitors' prices consistently. These businesses possess what we call an economy of scale.

Because of their large scale, in either production or purchase, the cost of production is much cheaper than their competitors'. These companies can comfortably lower their prices to a level that their competitors cannot duplicate if they want to stay profitable.

Imagine you want to set up a retail toy shop. You purchase toys from a supplier and sell them at a profit. A competing toy store has been in the market for years and has 50 retail shops all over the country. When both shops negotiate with a supplier, who do you think is likely to receive a bigger discount? You or your competitor who is purchasing 50 times more toys than you are? The answer is obvious. Suppliers will give more discount to your competitor because they cannot afford to offend or lose a big customer. As a result, your competitor can slash their prices to a point lower than yours and take away your customers.

Unless you can rapidly expand your business or find more customers so that you can increase your order with the supplier, you cannot compete with your competitor's pricing strategy. You will have to think of different ways to attract customers to survive in the game.

Most small retailers who are not able to differentiate themselves by means of unique products can only cross their fingers and pray. They will have to remain in special locations or provide special services to draw and retain customers. It will be difficult to survive because they are competing with businesses that have a durable competitive advantage known as economy of scale.

Amazon is the best example of this in the United States. They have huge networks and big bargaining power. Because of this, they can price everything from books to refrigerators more cheaply than their competitors. They make much more profit, can spend more on marketing, and can pay their employees more.

CHAPTER 20

Legal Barriers to Entry

Some companies have legal protection over their businesses. This includes legal contracts and government regulations. One example of government regulation is the Singapore Stock Exchange. According to the government, there can only be one stock exchange in the country, and thus it works like a monopoly.

If you want to list your company in the Singapore Exchange, you do not have any choices other than the Singapore Stock Exchange. In contrast, in the United States you have choices, whether it be the NYSE, the NASDAQ, etc.

Legal protection such as patents can raise barriers to entry for competitors. This is very evident in the pharmaceutical industry. Drug companies apply for patents for their products to protect their intellectual properties. During the patent protection period, competitors are not allowed to make, use, sell, or import the protected drugs without the inventor's consent. But patents expire. Once patents reach their expiration date, it becomes legal for competitors to "copy" these profitable inventions.

A good example is paracetamol, an analgesic used to treat minor aches and pains and reduce fevers. This drug was originally marketed as Tylenol, a very popular brand of Johnson

& Johnson. But after the expiration of the patent on paracetamol, brands such as Panadol and Feverall have taken part of Tylenol's market share.

So, while a patent can raise legal barriers for competitors to enter a market, it is very important for a business to use the protection period to build its brand in order to gain a foothold as a market leader.

CHAPTER 21

High Switching Costs

I have an acquaintance, Dennis, who is an inveterate Casanova. Very often he'll introduce a new girlfriend to us over lunch or dinner. Within a few weeks, we'll meet a different lady.

Dennis is careful not to get into any long-term commitments. *Marriage* is a taboo word to Dennis.

As long as he's not married, Dennis can flirt and switch girlfriends to his heart's content—that is to say, without engendering any significant monetary, emotional, or social consequences or costs.

In the business world, there are products and services that customers like us are, unknowingly, married to. As Warren says, "If you are going to buy a company, do so as if you were going to marry it. Forever."

An example is Microsoft Office software. If you want to change from Microsoft Office to another office suite, you need to purchase a new software package plus all the associated desktop applications, servers, and services. This is costly.

It would take a long time and require a lot of money to retrain people to use a new brand of software. And the new software might not be compatible with what clients and other companies are using, since most businesses are "married" to Microsoft Office.

Wrapping up

We have looked at four different types of Economic Moats: branding, economy of scale, legal barriers to entry, and high switching costs. Can you identify which durable competitive advantage each of the businesses you listed earlier may have?

Place your businesses into each of the four categories. At the same time, for additional practice, add in other possible businesses you can think of.

1. Branding

_____

_____

_____

_____

_____

_____

_____

2. Economy of Scale

_____

_____

_____

_____

_____

_____

_____

3. Legal Barriers to Entry

_____

_____

_____

_____

_____

_____

_____

_____

4. High Switching Costs

_____

_____

_____

_____

_____

_____

_____

These are just some examples of the possible Economic Moats. Before we conclude this chapter, there are two important things you must take note of.

1. Moats may not last forever.

Even the strongest brand can be threatened. Look at Walmart. Although the company has a strong economy of scale, its moat is under pressure due to the growing impact of e-commerce. As more and more people shop online, even the most profitable retail stores increasingly find their survival being threatened.

That being said, companies with huge moats do not vanish overnight, since people take time to get used to innovation and new products. Nevertheless, it is crucial to review your portfolio frequently (at least yearly) and determine if the businesses you have invested in will still be relevant ten years from now, and/or if you need to reconfigure your portfolio.

2. Some companies have multiple moats.

Another thing to note is that some companies have multiple moats. A company that has more than one moat, such as a branded name and a unique product, can raise its prices in any economy.

What is more important is that you understand that the business you are investing in has an advantage that you can identify with. This being the case, it is also true that if the advantage should cease to exist, you will be able to notice that, too.

SECRET 5

LANGUAGE OF BUSINESS

CHAPTER 22

Financial Statements Explained

"Excuse me, could you tell me how to get to Tokyo Tower?" I had been driving around the streets of Tokyo in circles for about an hour and still had no clue how to get to my destination. This was the first time I had visited Japan, way before Google Maps and Google Translate were available. I was, frankly, shocked that most Japanese couldn't speak English.

"*Nihongo ga hanasemasu ka?*" (Can you speak Japanese?) the gentleman replied.

"*Nihongo Wakarimasen.*" (I do not understand Japanese.) I replied with one of the few sentences I knew.

The gentleman went on to speak to me in Japanese for the next five minutes before bowing politely and leaving.

I felt so lost in a foreign land where I couldn't understand or speak the language.

To many, the stock market is like a foreign land where trained investors speak a foreign tongue. That's the reason why many lose their way in the stock market and wonder how they can ever reach their destination. The answer to this problem is to learn the language of investing. In the following chapters, Mary and I will be teaching you the language of business. You will be surprised how simple it can be once someone guides you through.

THE LANGUAGE OF BUSINESS

Accounting is the language of business. In this part of the book, we will look at three financial statements that allow you to assess businesses and reach educated conclusions about whether they are good investments.

We will look at three different types of businesses to help you to understand financial statements. The businesses are each run by one person:

1. Wong owns a restaurant.
2. Ahmed owns a tiny firm.
3. Jane runs a construction company.

They each have been running their business for years and have shareholders in the company. Every year the owners prepare financial statements for their shareholders, summarizing how the businesses are doing.

Note: Companies listed on a stock exchange are required to report their quarterly (every three months) or half-yearly results to the stock exchange in which they are listed, and these will be released to the public.

For our purposes, we will look at the annual (yearly) financial statements for each business.

There are three main financial statements:

1. Balance sheet
2. Income statement
3. Cash-flow statement

After you examine these statements carefully, you will be able to determine which business might be a good investment.

Where can you find the financial statements of companies?

Step 1: Do a Google search for that company's name.

Step 2: Go to that company's website.

Step 3: Search and click on a tab named "Investors' Relations."

Step 4: Search for presentations or annual reports.

Step 5: Open or download the annual reports.

Step 6: The annual reports will contain the three financial statements and additional details on the information written on the annual reports.

SHORTCUT METHOD

Do a Google search for "company's name + annual report." For example, search for "ABC Company annual report."

You will typically find the link to read the latest annual report. If you want to access all past reports, use the method described above.

CHAPTER 23

Balance Sheet

A balance sheet is a record of what a business owns and owes. To help us understand the balance sheet of a business, it may be useful to first understand that each of us also has a balance sheet. Let's think about what we own and what we owe personally. Take a moment and write down your balance sheet.

A balance sheet has three main segments:

1. Assets: things the business owns
2. Liabilities: things the business owes
3. Equity: also known as the business's net worth

To help you understand these terms better and how a balance sheet is prepared, I have asked my friend Tommy to share his personal balance sheet with you.

Let's look at Tommy's personal balance sheet to assess his financial health.

Tommy's personal balance sheet as of December 31, 2018			
Assets		**Liabilities**	
Current assets		**Current liabilities**	
Cash in bank	$3,000	Credit card bills	$500
iPhone	$1,000	Loan from mother-in-law	$2,000
Branded clothes	$500		
Laptop	$1,200	**Noncurrent liabilities**	
		House loan	$400,000
Noncurrent assets		Car loan	$7,000
Car	$10,000		
House	$500,000	**Total liabilities**	$409,500
Total assets	$515,700	**Equity**	$515,700
		Net worth	$106,200

First, we take a look at his assets. You can see that we differentiate between current assets and noncurrent assets. Typically, current assets are assets that will be used up or could very quickly be converted into cash within one year.

For discussion's sake, we have classified Tommy's latest iPhone, laptop, and branded clothes as current assets. The values that we have assigned to these items will be their estimated current values if we were to sell them off in the market immediately.

These values fluctuate and the cash amount is likely to change daily, which means that a balance sheet is a snapshot at a particular moment in time. For the purposes of this book, we will assume that this is what Tommy had on December 31, 2018.

We can see that Tommy's personal possessions are worth $515,700. This means that if Tommy were to sell off everything he has right now, he would receive an estimated amount of $515,700.

But don't forget that he also has liabilities: he owes money. As we can see, there are current liabilities and noncurrent liabilities.

Current liabilities must be paid back within a year or less (credit card bills and the loan he was given from his mother-in-law), whereas noncurrent liabilities are debts that can be repaid in more than one year.

So even though Tommy will receive $515,700 if he sells all his assets, we have to remember that he must pay back all his liabilities. His total liabilities are $409,500. That will leave him with $515,700 - $409,500 = $106,200.

This $106,200 is known as Tommy's *net worth*. In accounting terms, this portion of Tommy's balance sheet is known as *equity*. In summary:

Equity = Assets – Liabilities

Following, we reproduced the balance sheets of Wong, Ahmed, and Jane. Let's go through them one by one and you will soon find out how to understand each business.

Let's first take a look at the balance sheet for Wong's restaurant business.

Wong's restaurant balance sheet as of December 31, 2018			
Assets		**Liabilities**	
Current assets		**Current liabilities**	
Cash	$10,000	Accounts payable	$20,000
Inventory	$20,000	Term loan	$20,000
Accounts receivable	$10,000		
Noncurrent assets		**Noncurrent liabilities**	
Furniture	$50,000	Long-term debt	$30,000
Equipment	$30,000		
Total assets	**$120,000**	**Total liabilities**	**$70,000**
		Equity	
		Capital	$30,000
		Retained earnings	$20,000
		Total equity	**$50,000**

Once we look closely at Wong's balance sheet, the remaining businesses will be easier to understand.

First, let's take a look at the assets. Bear in mind that assets are what the business needs in order to operate.

Wong's Current Assets

Under current assets, we see cash, inventory, and accounts receivable.

Cash is money that is readily available. A restaurant needs cash in order to operate. The amount of cash a business collects is considered as part of its assets. Currently, Wong's restaurant has $10,000 cash. Some of it may be in the cash register and some may be in the bank. Some financial statements break the cash component down further into bank balances and petty cash (cash in hand).

Inventory refers to the products of a business. In Wong's case, inventory may include raw food such as meat, vegetables, noodles, and eggs. Currently, Wong has $20,000 worth of inventory. If he doesn't have enough customers patronizing his restaurant, all this raw food can spoil within a few days.

Accounts receivable is the money Wong expects to receive from his customers. Typically, restaurant customers pay on the spot, but in some cases, when his customers are corporate businesses, they may pay later, typically within 60 days. These delayed payments are known as accounts receivable. Wong has $10,000 worth of accounts receivable.

Wong's Noncurrent Assets

Furniture Wong bought for the restaurant is worth $50,000 based on the current estimate. He expects to use this furniture for at least the next five years, so it is considered a non-current asset.

Equipment refers to Wong's cooking utensils, cutlery, and dishes. These are worth an estimated $30,000. This value is based on an estimate of how much he could fetch if he resold this equipment on the market.

Note: How does Wong estimate the value of his furniture and equipment?

Typically, a business estimates the amount of time that they will use their assets, and then amortizes the cost of the assets. For example, if Wong bought 100 tables for $5,000 and he expects to use them for five years, the accounts will reflect that these 100 tables will decrease by a value of $5,000 divided by 5 years = $1,000 per year.

So in the first year, the tables will be reflected as being worth $5,000. In the second year, they will be worth $4,000. By the sixth year, they are virtually worthless. This is known as depreciation. (Different companies use different methods of determining depreciation depending on what is relevant to their business.)

We can see that in total, Wong's assets are worth $120,000. And we can assume we would need about $120,000 to set up a restaurant similar to Wong's.

This $120,000 can be financed by Wong in two possible ways:

1. Using his own money and injecting capital, or
2. By borrowing assets (money or other things needed).

Let's look at Wong's liabilities.

Wong's Current Liabilities

Accounts payable is money that Wong's business needs to pay his suppliers; hence the term *payable*. When Wong buys raw food from his suppliers every month, he has up to 60 days after the delivery of the raw food to make his payment.

The $20,000 shown on his balance sheet as accounts payable reflects the purchase of raw food, but Wong has not paid for this yet and must do it soon. Hence it is a liability.

Term loan of $20,000 consists of bank loans that have to be paid back during the current year. This loan was taken by Wong to buy equipment and furniture.

Wong's Noncurrent Liabilities

The $30,000 shown under long-term debt reflects debts that Wong has more than one year to pay back. As the debt term approaches one year, it will be considered short-term debt.

All in all, we see that Wong has total liabilities of $70,000, and $120,000 worth of assets are required to run the business. We can say that $70,000 of the assets are financed by debts and accounts payable.

Wong's Equity

Finally, we look at Wong's *equity*, which is the net worth of the business. Remember: Assets – Liabilities = Equity. Simply put, if we sell all of Wong's assets, we get $120,000, but we still need to pay Wong's $70,000 liabilities. After this deduction, the remaining amount is $50,000. This is the money that really belongs to Wong and his shareholders.

We can see that equity has two components on the balance sheet.

Capital is the amount of money contributed by Wong and his shareholders to start the business. You'll note $30,000 is the amount they put into the business.

Retained earnings of $20,000 are profits the business made previously that were invested in the company to continue to finance the business.

When Wong's business makes money, it can return the money either to the shareholders in the form of dividends, or he can retain the profits, which will be reflected in the balance sheet as retained earnings.

Now that we have gone through Wong's balance sheet, let's quickly look through Ahmed's and Jane's balance sheets.

By the end of this chapter, we will be discussing some key important ratios and things to take note of when looking at the balance sheet.

Ahmed's Consultancy balance sheet as of December 31, 2018			
Assets		**Liabilities**	
Current assets		**Current liabilities**	
Cash	$10,000	Accounts payable	$0
Inventories	$0	Short-term debts	$5,000
Accounts receivable	$10,000		
Shares of businesses	$30,000		
Noncurrent assets		**Noncurrent liabilities**	
Furniture	$5,000	Long-term debt	$10,000
Equipment	$5,000		
Total assets	**$60,000**	**Total liabilities**	**$15,000**
		Equity	
		Capital	$25,000
		Retained earnings	$20,000
		Total equity	**$45,000**

It is interesting to note that on Ahmed's balance sheet, there isn't any *inventory* or *accounts payable*.

When we asked Ahmed about this, he explained that since he runs a consultancy business, he doesn't have any inventory. He does not have to keep any products in the store (like Wong's raw foods) before they can be converted to cash.

This makes sense, since consultancy is a knowledge-based service. Ahmed's team of consultants visits clients to provide consultancy services. Since Ahmed doesn't have inventory and no suppliers whom he needs to pay, he has no accounts payable.

You can see the overall assets Ahmed needs for his business are $60,000. This is financed by $15,000 in liabilities and $45,000 in equity.

Jane's Construction balance sheet as of December 31, 2018			
Assets		**Liabilities**	
Current assets		**Current liabilities**	
Cash	$300,000	Accounts payable	$150,000
Inventories	$200,000	Short-term debts	$100,000
Accounts receivable	$200,000		
Noncurrent assets		**Noncurrent liabilities**	
Office equipment	$150,000	Long-term debts	$400,000
Equipment	$600,000		
Land	$500,000		
Total assets	**$1,950,000**	**Total liabilities**	**$650,000**
		Equity	
		Capital	$800,000
		Retained earnings	$500,000
		Total equity	**$1,300,000**

Jane is in the construction business. The assets required to run her business add up to millions of dollars. Her inventory is raw materials—steel, bricks, cement, and other materials needed for construction.

You will notice that Jane owns land worth $500,000 and expensive equipment such as trucks and machineries worth $600,000. The total value of Jane's assets is $1,950,000. This is financed by $650,000 in liabilities and $1,300,000 in equity.

We hope you are getting more familiar with the language of businesses and balance sheets. If you are new to accounting, we will go through the financial statements slowly and repeat certain important concepts to help you get familiar with the language.

Important Ratios and Numbers to Look at in the Balance Sheet

All the information in the balance sheet is important. However, there are a few vital pieces of information that will explain how the business is performing; we can extrapolate this information if we ask some basic questions:

1. Is the equity of the business growing over time?

    We want to have a business with net worth that increases over time. If we were to buy shares in a company, we want our business to become richer and richer. Net worth is a very direct way to gauge how well a business is doing. This is one of the key methods that Warren Buffett uses to assess his own business, Berkshire Hathaway.

    In the previous examples above, we only saw the current year's record. To get a full picture of the health of a company we also need to look for the past years' balance sheets. Are profits increasing? Is the debt decreasing?

2. Does the business have huge debt?

    Having a huge amount of debt is dangerous. When the economy or sector (such as the energy sector or the health care sector) doesn't do well, and the business is carrying huge debt, it can be very troublesome. This is because if the business is unable to finance the loan, the interest owed to the banks will roll over and compound and the debt amount will grow.

This is one of the main reasons companies go bankrupt. If you do not have huge debts, the possibility of going bankrupt is very low, isn't it?

Look at the three companies whose balance sheets we reviewed. You will see that the businesses have the following debt:

	Short-term	Long-term	Total debt
Wong	$20,000	$30,000	$50,000
Ahmed	$5,000	$10,000	$15,000
Jane	$100,000	$400,000	$500,000

What does this information tell us?

Some of us may conclude that Jane's construction company has much more debt than the other two businesses, so it is a dangerous business to invest in. That sounds reasonable. But we also have to understand how large the debt is relative to the size of the business.

To help you understand, let's use an example of two individuals, Ms. Greenfield and Ms. Priscilla. Ms. Greenfield has a personal debt of $30,000. Ms. Priscilla has a personal debt of $60 million. Who is in the more dangerous position?

At first glance, Ms. Priscilla's $60 million debt may cause some alarm. But here is an additional piece of information.

Ms. Greenfield is an 18-year-old with a net worth of $3,000. Ms. Priscilla is the wife of Mark Zuckerberg, whose combined net worth is estimated to be $60 billion (at the time of writing).

If you think about it:

Ms. Greenfield's debt ($30,000) is 1,000% more than her net worth ($3,000) while Ms. Priscilla's debt ($60 million) is only 0.1% of her net worth ($60 billion).

So what looks more dangerous now?

DEBT TO EQUITY

We used a ratio known as *debt to equity* to assess the risks of two businesses. We compared how much debt the person is holding with how much equity (net worth) the person has.

Let's apply the debt-to-equity ratio to the three businesses we started with and see how well these businesses are doing.

	Short-term debt	Long-term debt	Equity	Debt to equity
Wong	$20,000	$30,000	$50,000	100%
Ahmed	$5,000	$10,000	$45,000	33%
Jane	$100,000	$400,000	$1,300,000	38%

If you are wondering how we derived the debt-to-equity ratio in percentage, we took the total debt (short-term debt plus long-term debt) and divided it by the equity.

Total Debt ÷ Equity = Debt-to-Equity Ratio
Example: Jane's Construction
Total debt is ($100,000 + $400,000) = $500,000
Equity = $1,300,000
Debt to equity = $500,000 / $1,300,000 = 38%

Based on that information, we can see that the business with the highest debt relative to its equity is Wong's Restaurant.

A good debt-to-equity ratio is less than 50%.

Let's take Jane as an example. Even though her total debt is $500,000, we know that her business's net worth is $1,300,000. She has land and equipment that are worth more than her debt. This means she can probably pay off her debt easily by selling some of her assets.

When you examine a company's balance sheet, you may see items that we have yet to discuss in this book.

As businesses evolve, the types of assets or liabilities held by the company may be new or unfamiliar to you.

In order to understand each item on the balance sheet, you will need to read the notes attached to the annual report. Our general rule is that if the items on the balance sheet become too complex, we choose not to invest in the business.

CONCLUSION

There are two key things we look at in a company's balance sheet:

1. Is the equity (also known as book value) growing over the years?
2. Does the business have high debt? This is determined by looking at the current debt-to-equity ratio.

In the next few chapters, we will look at additional factors that help us choose businesses to invest in, and we will create a checklist.

CHAPTER 24

Income Statement

In this chapter, we will be looking at an even more exciting statement: the income statement. We say this is an exciting statement because it is the report card of a business.

The income statement allows us to see if the business is making money or losing money. Like a balance sheet, each of us has a personal income statement.

Let's bring our friend Tommy back into the picture and take a look at his income statement for 2018.

Tommy's income statement for year ending December 31, 2018	
Income	
Salary	$40,000
Part-time tuition	$12,000
Lucky dip at company's dinner and dance	$2,000
Dividends from stocks	$5,000
Total income	**$59,000**
Expenses	
Housing loan	$12,000
Transport	$10,000
Food	$7,000
Phone bills	$2,000
Bank interest	$2,000
Holiday	$5,000
Income taxes	$2,000
Total expenses	**$40,000**
Net income (savings)	**$19,000**

Your personal income statement summarizes the money you make, minus the money you spend in one year. What is left is the net amount you saved that year.

Wong's income statement for year ending December 31, 2018	
Income	
Revenue	$50,000
Cost of goods sold	$25,000
Gross profits	$25,000
Less expenses	
Rental	$7,000
Salary	$7,000
Depreciation	$2,000
Electrical bills	$1,000
Bank interest	$2,000
Total expenses	$19,000
Profit before tax	$6,000
Taxes	($1,000)
Net profit	$5,000

Now take a look at the business income statements for our three businesses. We will start with the performance of Wong's Restaurant for the entire year of 2018.

For ease of explanation and calculation, we've used modest numbers instead of millions of dollars.

Revenue is the amount of sales, or money collected from customers. In other words, Wong sold $50,000 worth of food in 2018.

Cost of goods sold is the cost of the materials Wong used

to produce the $50,000 worth of food he sold. If Wong sells noodles for $5 per plate and he sold 10,000 plates of noodles, he collected $50,000 from his customers.

For each plate of noodles sold, he estimates that the cost of the raw food used (noodles, eggs, meat, vegetables, etc.) is $2.50. Thus the cost of noodles sold that year is $2.50 x 10,000 plates = $25,000.

Wong's gross profit on 10,000 plates of noodles is $25,000. This profit is based purely on selling noodles and deducting the cost of producing the noodles.

If the gross profit is too small, the business will not be worth operating.

To calculate the true profit—known as *net profit*—we have to deduct Wong's other expenses, which consist of rent, salaries, depreciation, electrical bills, and bank interest.

In Wong's case, these expenses are $19,000.

Remember that there is a line on the balance sheet for depreciation. When Wong buys his equipment or furniture, he estimates how long these assets will be useful. For example, if Wong bought 100 tables for $5,000 and he expects to use them for 5 years, the accounts will reflect that these 100 tables decrease by a value of $5,000 divided by 5 years = $1,000 per year.

This $1,000 is known as *depreciation*—the decrease in value of the asset—and it will be expensed off the following year. Wong will also have to give an estimated depreciation value of the assets he bought, such as kitchen equipment and utensils. Although he has probably paid for these in full, he will not put the full depreciation amount into his income statement the year he bought them. Instead, he will expense them over five years. This will be a more accurate representation of his expenses. So if he bought the tables in 2019, instead of having a onetime $5,000 expense for table depreciation this year—2019—he will have a $1,000 expense for table depreciation for 2019, 2020, 2021, 2022, and 2023. Because he is spreading out the expenses, his yearly profit will also be more accurately represented instead of showing a onetime drop in the year he buys this furniture.

After deducting the total expenses of $19,000 from $25,000, we have $6,000. This is the *profit before tax*. Some investors use profit before tax to gauge the performance of a business. But in our opinion, good tax planning is an important part of the management's responsibilities. So we focus on net profit.

Net profit is the final amount of profit shareholders can expect to be considered theirs. This is the fruit of a business's labor for the year after all expenses and taxes are paid. Wong's Restaurant made a net profit of $5,000 in 2018. Is this considered a good profit? We will discuss this after looking at the other two businesses.

Ahmed's income statement for year ending December 31, 2018	
Income	
Revenue	$40,000
Cost of sales	$10,000
Gross profits	**$30,000**
Income from investments	$10,000
Less expenses	
Rental	$10,000
Salary	$5,000
Advertising	$5,000
Electrical bills	$1,000
Bank interest	$2,000
Total expenses	**$23,000**
Profit before tax	$17,000
Taxes	($2,000)
Net profit	**$15,000**

As we discussed, Ahmed's business is different from Wong's. Ahmed's consultancy business had $10,000 worth of cost of sales, which can be attributed to the external consultants he engaged and paid separately.

While he collected $40,000 in sales, he paid $10,000 to the consultants who helped to fulfill the services he had provided.

Another interesting thing to note is that Ahmed had *income from investments*. Ahmed explained that in the course of his work, he discovered some very good businesses and offered to invest in them.

If we look back at his balance sheet, we will see that Ahmed has listed shares of businesses as assets. Other than these two items—that is, income from investments and shares of stock—we see that he spent $5,000 on advertising. This is something we did not see in Wong's income statement.

Overall, we see that Ahmed made $15,000 in net profit for 2018.

Jane's income statement for year ending December 31, 2018	
Income	
Revenue	$4,000,000
Cost of goods sold	$2,000,000
Gross profits	**$2,000,000**
Less expenses	
Rental	$500,000
Salary	$320,000
Engineering services	$400,000
Electrical bills	$100,000
Bank interest	$80,000
Total expenses	**$1,400,000**
Profit before tax	$600,000
Taxes	($80,000)
Net profit	**$520,000**

Jane's construction business made a gross profit of $2,000,000 and a net profit of $520,000 after tax deductions.

In summary:

    Net profit of Wong's Restaurant   = $5,000
    Net profit of Ahmed's Consultancy = $15,000
    Net profit of Jane's Construction   = $520,000

So which business is the most profitable? The obvious answer is Jane's construction business.

CONSISTENCY OF PROFITS IS IMPORTANT

One important thing to consider is whether each business is consistent. Let's look at 10 years of net profit for each company to see how consistent it has been.

	Wong	Ahmed	Jane
2009	$4k	$300	$800k
2010	$4k	$500	-$500k
2011	$4.2k	$800	$20k
2012	$4.5k	$1k	$300k
2013	$4.5k	$3k	$10k
2014	$4.8k	$5k	-$300k
2015	$4.8k	$8k	$700k
2016	$5.2k	$10k	-$50k
2017	$5k	$12k	$300k
2018	$5k	$15k	$520k

NET PROFITS OF WONG, AHMED, AND JANE SINCE 2009

Based on the results of the past 10 years, we can draw the following conclusions:

Wong's business is relatively stable. Because it does not show much growth, we can assume that it is a mature business. That being said, since the restaurant has a profitable model, Wong could probably franchise this model or expand his restaurant. Think of McDonald's or KFC, and you'll be able to see how a profitable restaurant business can grow and expand worldwide. Of course, success depends largely on the ability of management to scale the business.

Ahmed's business, on the other hand, is growing. Profits grew from $300 in 2009 (probably just a part-time business at the time) to $15,000. The company was 50 times bigger in 2018 than it was 10 years earlier. It seems like Ahmed's consultancy business has the potential to continue to grow. Ahmed already employs external consultants and does not run the business all by himself; for this reason, we say that he has the mechanisms in place to hire staff as needed

Unlike the other two businesses, Jane's Construction is what we term a *cyclical business*. It does well and is profitable sometimes, and it loses money at other times. We observe that during the 10 years in question, it had losses in 2010, 2014, and 2016. Clearly, this company is less consistent than the other two we examined. As value investors, we may not want to invest in Jane's business because we may lose money some years . . . ouch!

EFFICIENCY OF BUSINESS

Another measure we look at is how efficient a business is in using the equity it retains. Remember: Equity is basically shareholders' money. (That is, our money!!!)

Equity is the money shareholders injected to start the business plus the amount of profit the company retained rather than distributing back to stockholders. If the company is not distributing money back to us, they'd better be making good use of it!

So how do we gauge if a business is making good use of its equity? Let's look at how much profit the company is making for us compared to the amount of equity they are keeping in the business.

Just to recap, the amount of equity in each of the three businesses for 2018 is:

Wong's Restaurant	= $50,000
Ahmed's Consultancy	= $45,000
Jane's Construction	= $1,300,000

If we want to see how efficiently the businesses have been using their equity in 2018, we should look at the equity they had on December 31, 2017; that was the equity they used to generate profit in 2018.

So we checked with the owners, and the amount of equity they had in 2017 was:

Wong's Restaurant	= $48,000
Ahmed's Consultancy	= $35,000
Jane's Construction	= $1,000,000

Now we want to see how well the companies used the equity they had at the beginning of the year. How much profit did they make as a percentage of equity? This is also known as *return on equity* (ROE).

	Equity in 2015	Profits in 2016	Return on equity for 2016
Wong	$48,000	$5,000	10.41%
Ahmed	$35,000	$15,000	42.85%
Jane	$1,000,000	$520,000	52%

As we can see, Jane's return on equity is the highest at 52%, followed by Ahmed's at 42.9% and Wong's at 10.4%.

As for profits, we want to check out each company's past results to have a better understanding of their performance. These are the results of the past 10 years:

Return on equity (ROE) of Wong, Ahmed, and Jane since 2009			
	Wong	Ahmed	Jane
2009	10.8%	50%	70%
2010	11.5%	52%	-52%
2011	12.3%	48%	18%
2012	11.6%	35%	30%
2013	10.5%	38%	5%
2014	11.5%	43%	-32%
2015	12%	38%	10%
2016	10%	39%	-48%
2017	11%	29%	30%
2018	10.41%	42.85%	52%

Generally speaking, a business that consistently has a ROE of 15% and above is an excellent business.

With the 10-year record shown above, we can see that Wong's ROE hovered between 10% and 12%. Ahmed's ROE ranged from 29% to 52%. Jane's ROE fluctuated from -52% to 70% due to the cyclical nature of her business.

Ahmed's ROE fluctuated quite a bit, but it is consistently high (almost always above 30%). Jane's business, on the other hand, fluctuated much too much.

As value investors, we tend to avoid businesses with such inconsistent ROE. We prefer predictable businesses so we can have predictable results.

Summary

Now when you look at an income statement, you can easily tell if the company is profitable.

Remember two key things:

1. The 10-year record of profits will be an accurate gauge of whether the business is making money.
2. The 10-year record of return on equity (ROE) will show us how efficient the business is in using its equity.

In the previous chapter, we also looked at two key indicators on the balance sheet:

1. Is the equity, a.k.a. book value, growing over time?
2. Look at the current debt-to-equity ratio to determine if the business has high debt.

Now we have four criteria we can use as the bases for our investment checklist.

S/No	Questions	Where to find
1	Check if the book value has been growing over the years.	Balance sheet
2	Check if the business has a reasonable debt by looking at the debt-to-equity ratio.	Balance sheet
3	Check 10 years of profits to see if the business is consistently profitable.	Income statement
4	Check 10 years of return on equity to see if the business has been efficiently managed.	Income statement and balance sheet

CHAPTER 25

Cash-Flow Statement

The *cash-flow statement* is the third important financial statement we consider when evaluating businesses. It tracks the amount of cash that flows in and out of the business for the current year. What does that mean?

Think of the cash-flow statement as your bank statement. It tracks the actual amount of cash that flows into and out of your account. Some of you may be thinking: How does that differ from the income statement in which the business collects money from customers and pays for expenses?

That's a good question. Here are possible explanations as to how a cash-flow statement may differ from the income statement:

1. The amount a business records as profit may not have been collected yet.

   Using our personal example, Tommy may have delivered $1,000 worth of tuition services in the month of March and recorded an income of $1,000 from tuition. But he will not receive the payment until April. In other words, although the income is recognized in March, the money may not have been received yet.

141

The three businesses we have examined all have accounts receivable. These are the amounts of money they expect to receive from their customers soon, depending on the terms they have agreed upon with their customers. Common business agreements can be 30 days, 90 days, even up to 180 days.

This means the businesses have already delivered the products or services promised and recorded the profit, but have yet to receive the money from their customers.

2. The amount you spent has not been paid yet.

Credit cards . . . anyone? Tommy may have bought his new laptop for $2,000 using his credit card. But he has not paid his credit card bill yet. So while he records having spent that $2,000, the money has not been taken from his account. In the business example, the funds will be stated as accounts payable.

The concept of recording profits and expenses during the statement period (typically prepared on a quarterly basis) regardless of whether cash has been collected or paid is known as *accrual basis* (pronounced "a-cruel-base-sis").

3. Capital the company collected or paid out may not affect the income statement.

There are some items that affect cash but not the income statement. For example, Tommy borrowed $2,000 from his mother-in-law and thus had an inflow of cash of $2,000. But we can see that this $2,000 is considered neither income nor an expense. However, the interest he has to pay will be an expense. Last we heard, Tommy's mother-in-law was a "sweet" lady who charged a 10% monthly interest rate . . .

We have shown you various scenarios where cash flows into and out of a business. In the cash-flow statement, businesses have divided these transactions into three categories. We will look at Wong's cash-flow statement to have a better understanding of exactly what a cash-flow statement entails.

Wong's Restaurant cash-flow statement for year ending December 31, 2018	
Cash flow from operating activities	
Net income	$5,000
Depreciation	$2,000
Receivables	($10,000)
Payables	$20,000
Taxes payable	$0
Net cash from operating activities	$17,000
Cash flow from investing activities	
Investment in equipment/furniture	($2,000)
Purchase/sales of investments	$1,000
Net cash used for investing activities	($1,000)

Cash flow from financing activities	
Repayment of bank loan	($1,000)
Issue of dividends	($1,000)
Net cash used for financing activities	($2,000)
Net increase in cash	$14,000

To see how cash flow, income statement, and balance sheet are all related, we have brought Wong's income statement and balance sheet back into this chapter for quick and easy reference.

Wong's Restaurant income statement for year ending December 31, 2018	
Income	
Revenue	$50,000
Cost of goods sold	$25,000
Gross profits	$25,000
Less expenses	
Rental	$7,000
Salary	$7,000
Depreciation	$2,000
Electrical bills	$1,000
Bank interest	$2,000
Total expenses	$19,000
Profit before tax	$6,000
Taxes	($1,000)
Net profit	$5,000

Wong's Restaurant balance sheet as of December 31, 2018			
Assets		**Liabilities**	
Current assets		Current liabilities	
Cash	$10,000	Accounts payable	$20,000
Inventories	$20,000	Short-term debts	$20,000
Accounts receivable	$10,000		
Noncurrent assets		Noncurrent liabilities	
Furniture	$50,000	Long-term debt	$30,000
Equipment	$30,000		
Total assets	$120,000	Total liabilities	$70,000
		Equity	
		Capital	$30,000
		Retained earnings	$20,000
		Total equity	$50,000

Let's take a look at each entry on Wong's cash-flow statement.

Operating activities: This portion shows the income statement (profit and loss) on a cash basis instead of accrual basis. By looking at the operating activities, we can see the actual amount of cash flowing into and out in one year of the business operations. Wong's net income of $5,000 is taken from his income statement.

But bear in mind that some items recorded in the income statement may not reflect actual cash transactions.

Depreciation is the amount that Wong expensed for his

long-term assets such as tables, chairs, and kitchen equipment. He paid in cash when he bought these and estimated that they would be in usable condition for five years.

Therefore he divided the amount paid by five years and expensed that amount every year for five years rather than taking the total amount in one year.

Wong recorded $2,000 worth of depreciation in his income statement. This was for furniture and equipment he paid $10,000 for back in 2016. He already spent $10,000 fully in cash and is expensing the amount over five years. Hence this amount of $2,000 did not really involve cash that year. Cases such as this are known as noncash expenses. What this means is that although we see that Wong has a profit of $5,000, this amount is net of deducting all expenses including the $2,000 of depreciation, which is a noncash expense. So we need to understand that depreciation expenses do not affect cash flow.

Receivables are money that Wong expects to collect from his customers. He has recorded $10,000 worth of revenue in his income statement, but has not really collected the cash yet. This amount has to be deducted from the cash-flow statement because the $5,000 worth of profit includes this amount being recorded as revenue.

You can see that $10,000 worth of receivables are recorded in the balance sheet as *assets*. This is money that Wong expects to collect from customers. The invoices that he holds are considered as real monetary value.

Payables, on the other hand, refers to money that Wong expects to pay his suppliers. We can see that he deducted $25,000 worth of cost of goods sold in his income statement.

But he added back $20,000 worth of payables in his cash-flow statement. Why? Let's go through this step-by-step.

In the process of operating its daily business, Wong's Restaurant may have already used some products and services provided by his suppliers that Wong has an agreement to pay off later. In 2018, the supplier sent $20,000 worth of raw food to Wong's Restaurant. Wong then cooked the raw food to serve his customers. So in his income statement, he incurred $20,000 of expenses.

However, because Wong has not actually paid the supplier, he owes the supplier $20,000. The amount of money he owes is known as *payables*. Why did he add $20,000 back into the cash-flow statement then?

In the cash-flow statement, Wong started off with the amount of $5,000 as net income. However, in the income statement, $20,000 was deducted as an expense. In fact, the $20,000 has not been paid yet. Wong added back that amount to determine the amount of net cash still available.

If you find that this information is still a bit too abstract to digest, don't worry. We will summarize everything and suggest some important areas you should focus on. The next two subjects we will address are more straightforward. Let's take a look at them.

Investing activities: This portion of the cash-flow statement reports the buying and selling of long-term investments—in Wong's case, equipment.

We can see that in 2018, there was $2,000 of outflow to purchase new equipment and furniture. We can also see that there was an inflow of $1,000 from the sale of investments.

The inflow of money was due to Wong's selling off investments held by the business. People often ask, "What is the difference between investing activities and operating activities?" Isn't purchasing new kitchen equipment considered an operating activity rather than an investing activity?

Think of it this way: Do Wong's day-to-day operations consist of buying and selling kitchen equipment? The answer is no. His daily operations are producing food, selling food, and running the restaurant.

Financing activities: This portion records activities related to how Wong finances the business. This can be accomplished by raising funds from shareholders or borrowing from a bank. We can see that Wong had two activities in this category in 2018.

There is a $1,000 outflow of cash in repayment of debt. This means he paid off $1,000 of debt during this period. We can also see a $1,000 outflow in the issuance of dividends. Great news to shareholders, as they were given dividends this year!

CASH IS KING

In any business, cash is very important. And it is important to look at the cash-flow statement when we are deciding whether to invest in the business.

There are two important areas we zoom in on in the cash-flow statement:

1. Net cash from operating activities
2. Free cash flow

Net Cash from Operating Activities

Net cash from operating activities shows us whether there is cash coming in from operating the business.

We want to see consistent cash flow from the operations, because it will be a reflection that there is actual cash collected from the day-to-day operations of the business.

Let's take a look at the cash flow from operating activities for the three businesses for the past 10 years.

Net cash from operating activities of Wong, Ahmed, and Jane since 2009			
	Wong	Ahmed	Jane
2009	$3k	-$100	$750k
2010	$5k	-$400	-$400k
2011	$4.2k	-$200	$40k
2012	$4.1k	-$1k	$330k
2013	$3.5k	$3.3k	$12k
2014	$5.8k	$5.2k	-$250k
2015	$2.8k	$7.5k	$600k
2016	$6.2k	$9.2k	-$90k
2017	$6k	$11.4k	$350k
2018	$4k	$16k	$620k

Looking at the track records of the three businesses, we can observe the following:

1. Wong's business has very consistent cash flow, like his profits. We would say that his business is a

cash-producing business. We also noticed from his cash-flow statement that he paid dividends. So this is likely a *dividend play* in our investment portfolio.

This means we probably would invest in Wong's business and buy his shares in order to collect dividends.

2. Ahmed's business is very interesting; we can observe in its earlier years, from 2009 to 2012, that he actually had a negative cash flow from operations. This is very abnormal, as he had shown that he was making profits in these years.

Let's pull the 10-year profit records back here for easy reference.

Net profits of Wong, Ahmed, and Jane since 2009			
	Wong	Ahmed	Jane
2009	$4k	$300	$800k
2010	$4k	$500	-$500k
2011	$4.2	$800	$20k
2012	$4.5	$1k	$300k
2013	$4.5	$3k	$10k
2014	$4.8	$5k	-$300k
2015	$4.8	$8k	$700k
2016	$5.2	$10k	-$50k
2017	$5k	$12k	$300k
2018	$5k	$15k	$520k

We see that Ahmed had been making profits from 2009 all the way to 2018. But why was there negative cash flow from operating activities?

When we asked him about it, Ahmed explained that when he started his business in 2009, the deals he clinched were with smaller customers, many of whom did not pay him for his services. In 2013, he began to do things differently.

First, he began to look for bigger clients, and as he had had some years of experience by then, he was able to clinch deals with these clients.

Second, he also stated his payment terms up front with his customers so that he could get paid while he was doing the job and not at the completion of it.

For listed companies, we can find some of this information in the notes provided by the company in their annual report.

Alternatively, we can attend a company's general meeting, which is held once a year to give shareholders the opportunity to interact with and pose questions to the management of the company so that they can clarify any doubts they may have about it.

For Jane's business, we see that cash flow fluctuates, just like her profits, as she is in a cyclical business. Note that there are some excellent businesses that can produce relatively consistent profits and cash flow even in a cyclical business environment. It is likely that these businesses have a strong recurring component in their operations and a strong economic moat.

Free Cash Flow

The second item we look at is the *free cash flow* of the business. This is the amount of cash that is available for us, the shareholders, after all key expenses. What does this really mean?

This simply means if we stop the business now and reach our hands in to grab all the cash we are legally entitled to, the free cash flow will be that amount.

We will not go deeply into the calculation portion and the accounting terms of free cash flow since many financial websites actually calculate this number for us. We also fear that some of you may decide to burn this book in frustration if we go into overly technical details.

For more detailed explanations, you can simply Google "free cash flow."

Here is a simple explanation for free cash flow:

Net cash from operating activities – capital expenditures (necessary expenses to maintain current assets)

Note that there are many variations and details when it comes to free cash flow. So what is important is to understand the principle and how to interpret it.

Free cash flow: Wong, Ahmed, and Jane since 2009			
	Wong	Ahmed	Jane
2009	$2.5k	-$200	$650k
2010	$4.3k	-$500	-$500k
2011	$3.2k	-$400	$30k
2012	$3.5k	-$1.2k	$210k
2013	$2.8k	$2.3k	$9.2k
2014	$4.3k	$4.2k	-$280k
2015	$2.3k	$7.2k	$480k
2016	$5.2k	$8.1k	-$98k
2017	$5.4k	$9.4k	$280k
2018	$3.5k	$12k	$520k

You might have noticed that the numbers from free cash flow will mirror those from the net cash from operating activities unless there is huge capital expenditure. A company with a need for huge capital expenditure is not a very easy business to run.

Using a huge part of your cash to maintain the assets of the business can be very draining and stressful.

SUMMARY

In summary, we have looked at all three financial statements and can form a checklist to assess the business.

Investment checklist		
S/No	Item	Yes/No
1	Is equity (book value) growing over the past 10 years?	A growing equity is akin to a growing net worth of a company.
2	Is the latest debt-to-equity ratio less than 50%?	A business with a debt to equity indicates that it is conservatively financed.
3	Are the profits growing over the past 10 years?	We want to invest in businesses that have a good 10 years record of stable and growing profits.
4	Is the return on equity consistently high (more than 15%) over the past 10 years?	A high ROE indicates that the management of the company had been efficient.
5	Is the free cash flow of the company positive over the past 10 years? We want to invest in companies with more "Yeses."	A consistently positive free cash flow indicates that the company has sufficient cash to operate.

SECRET 6

VALUATION

CHAPTER 26

What Is Valuation?

The ability to valuate an investment is the core skill of any value investor. Interestingly, when I was a full-time army officer, I learned the importance of valuating opportunities, given the limited resources my fellow soldiers and I had in the military.

"Please send air support when we step into the enemy area!" I requested on one occasion.

"We do not waste our artillery rounds on foot soldiers. We go for high-payoff targets," one of the artillery officers told me.

"What do you mean 'high payoff'?" I asked.

"We have limited ammunition," the officer replied, "so it's important to use it wisely. Our goal is to damage the targets that have higher firepower. We determine which target can do more damage to us and which target is more difficult to destroy. Then we do weapons-to-enemy matching to ensure that we don't use our rounds on foot soldiers. The payoff is too low."

For those of us who are investors, cash is our ammunition: our bullets and missiles. Given our resources, we have to fire at high-payoff targets. The way to do that is to understand which stocks give the highest returns on investments.

In this part of the book, Mary and I are going to share how we use simple yet powerful methods to decide when we should, if you will, pull the trigger and buy a stock.

THE SECRET OF STOCK VALUATION

The key idea of value investing is to purchase an investment for less than its true value; in this way you capture value while buying the stock.

Imagine you are able to buy a dollar with only 50 cents.

How many dollars will you buy?

The answer will likely be "as many as possible."

This technique was developed by Benjamin Graham and David Dodd of Columbia Business School in the 1920s. In this segment, we will examine different valuation techniques that investors use.

As you learn about the different valuation methods, note that all methods are not suitable for all types of businesses.

Now it's time to equip yourself with one of the most powerful skills you can develop in the financial world.

CHAPTER 27

Graham's Net-Net

Benjamin Graham, the father of value investing, used a conservative valuation method called Net-Net. The principles of value investing were derived from this valuation model.

THE KEY IDEA OF NET-NET

The key idea of Net-Net is to first calculate how much shareholders would get back if the company stopped operating and returned all its money to them. This situation is known as liquidation. It reminds me of a not-so-funny joke, actually . . .

"Who was the most successful investor in history?" the joke begins.

The answer: "Noah. While the entire world was in liquidation, he managed to keep stocks above water."

Okay, not so funny. Anyway, the idea is to be able to purchase a stock below its liquidation value. If you manage to do that, you will be laughing all the way to the bank.

To purchase a stock for less than its true value, we need to:

1. Calculate the liquidation value
2. Buy the stock at a margin of safety (buy at a buffer below two thirds of its value)

CALCULATING NET CURRENT ASSET VALUE

So how do we know how much we will get back if the company goes into liquidation? The conservative method used by Benjamin Graham was to calculate what is known as net current asset value (NCAV). Let me explain this in layman terms.

As we discussed in chapter 23, a company's balance sheet tells us what the company owns and owes at a particular point in time. The balance sheet will tell us how much we will get back if the company closes down.

Net current assets = current assets – total liabilities

Using the three companies we looked at earlier, we can see how NCAV is derived. Note that some businesses have negative NCAV. In other words, the current assets of those businesses are less than their total liabilities. Net-Net investing is not a suitable technique for these companies.

Wong's Restaurant balance sheet as of December 31, 2018			
Assets		**Liabilities**	
Current assets		**Current liabilities**	
Cash	$10,000	Accounts payable	$20,000
Inventories	$20,000	Short-term debts	$20,000
Accounts receivable	$10,000		
Noncurrent assets		**Noncurrent liabilities**	
Furniture	$50,000	Long-term debt	$30,000
Equipment	$30,000		
Total assets	**$120,000**	**Total liabilities**	**$70,000**
		Equity	
		Capital	$30,000
		Retained earnings	$20,000
		Total equity	**$50,000**

Current assets = cash ($10,000) + inventories ($20,000) + accounts receivable ($10,000) = $40,000

Total liabilities = $70,000

Net current assets = $40,000 – $70,000 = -$30,000 (negative NCAV)

Ahmed's Consultancy balance sheet as of December 31, 2018			
Assets		**Liabilities**	
Current assets		**Current liabilities**	
Cash	$10,000	Accounts payable	$0
Inventories	$0	Short-term debts	$5,000
Accounts receivable	$10,000		
Shares of business	$30,000		
Noncurrent assets		**Noncurrent liabilities**	
Furniture	$5,000	Long-term debt	$10,000
Equipment	$5,000		
Total assets	**$60,000**	**Total liabilities**	**$15,000**
		Equity	
		Capital	$25,000
		Retained earnings	$20,000
		Total equity	**$45,000**

Current assets = cash ($10,000) + inventories ($0) +
accounts receivable ($10,000) + shares of businesses =
$50,000

Total liabilities = $15,000

Net current assets = $50,000 - $15,000 = $35,000

Jane's Construction balance sheet as of December 31, 2018			
Assets		**Liabilities**	
Current assets		**Current liabilities**	
Cash	$300,000	Accounts payable	$150,000
Inventories	$200,000	Short-term debts	$100,000
Accounts receivable	$200,000		
Noncurrent assets		**Noncurrent liabilities**	
Office equipment	$150,000	Long-term debt	$400,000
Equipment	$600,000		
Land	$500,000		
Total assets	**$1,950,000**	**Total liabilities**	**$650,000**
		Equity	
		Capital	$800,000
		Retained earnings	$500,000
		Total equity	**$1,300,000**

Current assets = cash ($300,000) + inventories ($200,000)
+ accounts receivable ($200,000) = $700,000
Total liabilities = $650,000
Net current assets = $700,000 - $650,000 = $50,000

So, after calculating, we can see the following:

NCAV of Wong's Restaurant = -$30,000
NCAV of Ahmed's Consultancy = $35,000
NCAV of Jane's Construction = $50,000

From the examples, we can see that Wong's Restaurant is not a good candidate for purchasing using the Net-Net approach because it has a negative NCAV. Let's look at Ahmed's and Jane's businesses.

One more step we need to take is to determine the NCAV *per share*. You have learned how to calculate the NCAV of a business; now it's time to learn how to calculate the NCAV per share.

Let's assume that Wong, Ahmed, and Jane have partners and other shareholders in their businesses. We look at the number of outstanding shares; this is the total number of shares held by all the shareholders, including big institutions such as banks and also the company's management and employees.

After talking to Wong, Ahmed, and Jane, we learned that they had the following:

Outstanding shares of Wong's Restaurant = 10,000
Outstanding shares of Ahmed's Consultancy = 35,000
Outstanding shares of Jane's Construction = 20,000

We divide the NCAV of each business by the number of outstanding shares to determine the NCAV per share:

NCAV per share of Wong's Restaurant = -$3
NCAV per share of Ahmed's Consultancy = $1
NCAV per share of Jane's Construction = $2.5

There we have it: our first valuation using Benjamin Graham's Net-Net model. But wait a minute. What should we do to make sure we can profit from the valuation? The answer: we should purchase a stock when it is undervalued. We can achieve this if we buy the stock at a share price under the NCAV per share. If we can buy shares of Ahmed's Consultancy at below $1 or shares of Jane's Construction at below $2.50, the transaction will be considered an undervalue deal.

In *The Intelligent Investor*, Benjamin Graham explained the concept of margin of safety. Many investors regard this as the most important aspect of investing.

According to Graham:

> To have a true investment there must be present a true margin of safety. And a true margin of safety is one that can be demonstrated by figures, by persuasive reasoning, and by reference to a body of actual experience.

MARGIN OF SAFETY

So, you ask, how do we find investments with a true *margin of safety*? The answer: we buy stock at a discounted price. If we want to use Graham's Net-Net technique successfully, we want to pay two thirds of the NCAV or less, regardless of the business type. In other words, we want a 33.3% (one third) discount before we are willing to buy the stock. Let's use Ahmed's Consultancy as an example.

The NCAV per share is $1. If we want to get a one-third (or 33.3%) discount, we will only be willing to pay $0.66 ($1 x 0.66).

Visually, it looks like this:

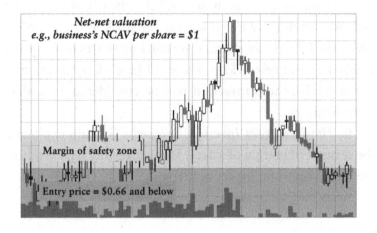

As you can see, the Net-Net valuation method is very conservative. We give ourselves a huge margin of safety so that even if the company closes today, we will still make money.

But things can still go wrong if you're using this valuation method. If a company loses money but chooses not to close down, its assets will run dry over time, and this will cause the net current asset value to drop below our original entry price. That is why it's important to choose a business that you have confidence in, no matter how safe the valuation method you use may seem. This is what Warren calls keeping within your circle of competence. Hence, when we look into his portfolio, we see that he holds on to businesses that he understands, businesses such as Coca-Cola and American Express. For years, Warren avoided technology stocks when many other investors were rushing to buy them because, as he said, he did not understand them well enough to acquire a stake in them.

CHAPTER 28

Price-to-Book Value

This second valuation method is a variation of Net-Net. Using price-to-book value is much simpler since many financial websites precalculate it for investors. Despite this, we should still understand what price-to-book value means and how to determine it.

THE KEY IDEA OF PRICE-TO-BOOK VALUE

The key idea of *price-to-book value* is to buy good businesses below their net asset value, which is known as book value or equity. If we look back at the balance sheet, we have the assets and the liabilities, and we also have the equity, the net worth of the business.

To help make things as clear as possible, remember that whenever you see the following terms, they mean the same thing.

Net asset value (NAV) = book value = equity = net worth of business

When we use price-to-book value to valuate a business for entry points, the idea again is to buy below the net asset value of the business. Similar to net current asset value, the net asset value is the amount of money shareholders get back if the company shuts down. The only difference is that instead of taking only the current assets, we include the noncurrent assets as well, since technically speaking, the noncurrent assets belong to the shareholders, too.

Net current asset value is a much more conservative valuation than price-to-book value because noncurrent assets such as furniture, land, and equipment may take a longer time to sell off. Also, the value we get back after selling them may not be comparable to what we initially assessed them to be. Imagine having to sell off your car, your house, or your shop immediately before you close your business. The chances of getting a good price are not very high.

Price-to-book value is the method used most often by accountants and investment firms, and thus it is easier to find on websites.

Before we calculate price-to-book value, let me share a story. A woman boasted to her friends, "My husband is a multimillionaire. And I'm confident that the reason for his current wealth is largely me." Her friends eventually got fed up with this conceited tone and asked, "So if you're so indispensable to his wealth, does it mean that he loves you?" The woman replied, "I'm not sure. Before he met me, he was a multi*billionaire*."

This story reminds us that the net worth of a business, like the net worth of a person, can drop if the business's or person's wealth is not well managed. This is why we must always implement the margin of safety.

So how do we use price-to-book value, and how do we add a margin of safety? First, using Wong's, Ahmed's, and Jane's businesses as examples, let's determine the businesses' net asset value (or book value, or equity).

Wong's Restaurant balance sheet as of December 31, 2018			
Assets		**Liabilities**	
Current assets		**Current liabilities**	
Cash	$10,000	Accounts payable	$20,000
Inventories	$20,000	Short-term debts	$20,000
Accounts receivable	$10,000		
Noncurrent assets		**Noncurrent liabilities**	
Furniture	$50,000	Long-term debt	$30,000
Equipment	$30,000		
Total assets	$120,000	Total liabilities	$70,000
		Equity	
		Capital	$30,000
		Retained earnings	$20,000
		Total equity	$50,000

The balance sheet shows that the equity for Wong's Restaurant is $50,000.

Ahmed's Consultancy balance sheet as of December 31, 2018			
Assets		**Liabilities**	
Current assets		**Current liabilities**	
Cash	$40,000	Accounts payable	$0
Inventories	$0	Short-term debts	$5,000
Accounts receivable	$10,000		
Noncurrent assets		**Noncurrent liabilities**	
Furniture	$5,000	Long-term debt	$10,000
Equipment	$5,000		
Total assets	**$60,000**	**Total liabilities**	**$15,000**
		Equity	
		Capital	$25,000
		Retained earnings	$20,000
		Total equity	**$45,000**

Total equity for Ahmed's Consultancy is $45,000.

Jane's Construction balance sheet as of December 31, 2018			
Assets		**Liabilities**	
Currents assets		Current liabilities	
Cash	$300,000	Accounts payable	$150,000
Inventories	$200,000	Short-term debts	$100,000
Accounts receivable	$200,000		
Noncurrent assets		Noncurrent liabilities	
Office equipment	$150,000	Long-term debts	$400,000
Equipment	$600,000		
Land	$500,000		
Total assets	$1,950,000	Total liabilities	$650,000
		Equity	
		Capital	$800,000
		Retained earnings	$500,000
		Total equity	$1,300,000

Total equity for Jane's Construction is $1,300,000.

After checking the balance sheets, we see the following:

NAV of Wong's Restaurant = $50,000
NAV of Ahmed's Consultancy = $45,000
NAV of Jane's Construction = $1,300,000

Now we need to find out what the *NAV per share* is. We refer to the number of outstanding shares.

Outstanding shares of Wong's Restaurant = 10,000
Outstanding shares of Ahmed's Consultancy = 35,000
Outstanding shares of Jane's Construction = 20,000

And we divide the NAV of each business by the outstanding shares in order to get:

NAV per share of Wong's Restaurant = $5
NAV per share of Ahmed's Consultancy = $1.29
NAV per share of Jane's Construction = $65

As you can see, the NAV per share of these businesses significantly increased when we considered the noncurrent assets, which may be significantly high in value. For example, in the case of Jane's Construction, Jane has land, buildings, etc.

As mentioned earlier, we need to define a margin of safety. We want to purchase a stock only when it has at least a 20% discount off the NAV per share. Thus, in the three examples above, our entry point for each will be as follows:

Taking 20% off the NAV per share for each business, we will be purchasing the businesses at a maximum 80% of their NAV. (Since we want 20%, we will only be willing to pay 80%.)

Entry price for Wong's Restaurant = $5 x 0.8 = $4
Entry price for Ahmed's Consultancy = $1.29 x 0.8 = $1.03
Entry price for Jane's Construction = $65 x 0.8 = $52

There are two things to note before we finish this part of the book. First, the term we use is price-to-book value (or NAV). And when we use websites to look for undervalued stocks, we will search for stocks with a price-to-book value that is 0.8 or lower.

Let me explain. When we use the term *price*, it means the stock price; when we use the term *book*, in this case, it means book value (or NAV) per share.

Let's use Wong's Restaurant as an example. We want to buy shares in Wong's business when its price-to-book value is 0.8 or lower.

Price/book ≤ 0.8

Since the book value per share of Wong's is $5, the equation becomes:

Price/$5 ≤ 0.8

Bringing $5 to the other side of the equation, we get:

Price ≤ 0.8x$5

Therefore, our game plan is to buy Wong's shares when:

Price ≤ $4

This is how we calculate the entry price of $4 for Wong's Restaurant, which is what we mentioned earlier. The reason we convert this into price-to-book value is that most financial websites present the information in this form.

So when we see that price-to-book is 0.8 or lower, we know that the stock is at an entry price we want. For example, if we see price/book (P/B) is 0.6 for Wong's Restaurant, it means the share price is currently 60% of its book value. This is considered a good discount of 40%.

The second thing we need to note is that not all companies need to have a lot of assets in order to operate. This makes it virtually impossible to buy these companies below book value.

For example, if we were to compare Ahmed's Consultancy with Jane's construction business, it is unlikely that we would be able to purchase Ahmed's company below book value because Ahmed's business is service-based and does not need huge assets to operate.

We gathered some information about popular stocks as a reference. Let's look at these.

Calculate the price-to-book ratio for each of them (June 2018 data).

Name	Business type	Price	Book value	Price/ book
Google	Online media	$970.12	$209.64	
Facebook	Online media	$149.60	$21.46	
Prudential Financial Inc.	Insurance	$107.75	$109.05	
Bank of America	Bank	$23.67	$24.41	

Here are the price/book ratios.

Name	Business type	Price	Book value	Price/book
Google	Online media	$970.12	$209.64	4.63
Facebook	Online media	$149.60	$21.46	6.97
Prudential Financial Inc.	Insurance	$107.75	$109.05	0.99
Bank of America	Bank	$23.67	$24.41	0.97

As you can see, it is very unlikely that we will be able to purchase an online media company such as Google or Facebook below its book value. The reason is that these businesses are valued primarily on their ability to produce profits and to grow.

On the other hand, it is more likely that we will be able to purchase insurance companies and banks below their book value because these companies require more equity—in this case cash—to run profitably. Warren has shares in many profitable insurance companies and banks, such GEICO, General Reinsurance, Torchmark, Bank of America, Wells Fargo, and Goldman Sachs.

So we only use price-to-book to evaluate companies that require many physical assets in their day-to-day operations. We will discuss other types of businesses in chapters 29 to 31.

CHAPTER 29

PE Ratio

The price-to-earnings ratio is another tool that is often used to determine if a company offers good value to investors. Here, instead of valuing a company based on its asset value, we look at it based on its earnings ability, its *price to earnings* (PE).

THE KEY IDEA OF PRICE-TO-EARNINGS (PE) RATIO

The goal is to break even on our investments as soon as possible, by not paying too high a price for a business in relation to how much the business is capable of earning.

Let's use Wong's Restaurant as an example. Here is his income statement again.

Wong's Restaurant income statement for year ending December 31, 2018	
Income	
Revenue	$50,000
Cost of goods sold	$25,000
Gross profits	$25,000
Less expenses	
Rental	$7,000
Salary	$7,000
Depreciation	$2,000
Electrical bills	$1,000
Bank interest	$2,000
Total expenses	$19,000
Profit before tax	$6,000
Taxes	($1,000)
Net profit	$5,000

We have seen that Wong's Restaurant makes $5,000 in a year. Hence, the "earnings" from the business is $5,000. If we were to make an offer to purchase the business, this would be known as the "price" we want to pay.

Let's assume we want to offer $50,000 for Wong's business, but Wong counteroffers a price of $100,000 (of course he wants more for his business). The two different prices can be looked upon as having two different PE ratios.

At a price of $50,000, Wong's business produces $5,000 of earnings; hence the PE ratio is

$50,000/$5,000 = 10 times the earnings, or PE of 10

In other words, we can expect to wait 10 years to break even on our investment if we pay $50,000 at a PE of 10.

At a price of $100,000, Wong's business still produces $5,000 of earnings; hence the PE ratio in this case is

$100,000/$5,000 = 20 times the earnings, or PE of 20.

In this case, we expect it to take 20 years for the company to break even. Now comes the important question: Would you invest in the business at 10 x PE or 20 x PE?

What Is a Good PE?

All things being equal, let's say we want to buy a company with a PE that is as low as possible, indicating that the business will need less time to break even than a company with a higher PE. One thing to note is that businesses from different industries are expected to grow at different rates. For example, the technology sector has been growing much faster than traditional brick and mortar sectors. These growth rates affect the industry's PE ratio. When the market expects the industry to grow faster, they are also willing to pay a higher PE to buy the business.

As of June 2018, these are the average PE ratios for each industry:

Sector	P/E
Energy	-38.5
Financial Services	16
Consumer Defensive	19.9
Industrials	21.9
Utilities	35.2
Consumer Cyclical	22.2
Basic Materials	36
Health Care	21.5
Communication Services	20.3
Technology	26.3
Real Estate	22.6
S&P 500	25.7

We can see that financial services has a lower PE on average than other industries. Utilities had the highest PE as of June 2018. Energy had a negative PE ratio. This was because many oil and gas companies lost money during this period and hence had negative earnings.

We want to find good investments in industries with a lower, or even negative, PE. But remember that the investments must fall within your circle of competence or interest.

We also have to determine what constitutes a good PE number for entering into an investment. A relatively safe position is to buy a stock with a PE that is 30% below the average PE.

For example, when we look at Visa's PE ratio for the past

10 years, we can see from the table that on average, the company's ratio for the past 10 years is 29.62.

	Visa
2009	25.88
2010	16.7
2011	19.7
2012	42.2
2013	29.3
2014	30.4
2015	30.06
2016	31.4
2017	40.72
2018	29.85
Avg.	29.62

So a good PE ratio to invest in Visa will be: 29.62 x 0.7 = 20.73.

How do we know when Visa has hit a PE ratio of 20.73? First we check the *earnings per share (EPS)* of the company.

EPS, simply put, is the total profit of a company divided by its number of outstanding shares. To calculate book value per share, we look for the earnings each share is entitled to, rather than the book value.

Checking Visa's EPS on the Internet, we see the EPS is currently $4.65. So I might buy into the company when its share price hits $4.65 x 20.73 = $96.39.

Let's review how to use PE ratios.

Step 1: Look for the average historical PE ratio by searching the Internet. Example: Visa's average is 29.62.

Step 2: Take 30% of the average PE to ensure that you have a margin of safety. Multiply Visa's average PE of 29.62 by 0.7 to get 20.73. This is the PE ratio that is 30% below the company's average.

Step 3: Look for the current earnings per share (EPS). Visa's current EPS is $4.65.

Step 4: Multiply the EPS by the discounted PE to get the entry price. Visa's EPS is $4.65; we multiply it by 20.73 to get $96.39.

So if Visa's price falls to $96.39 or below, we might grab it. Currently, the stock market is high. Visa's stock price is much higher than our target entry price. So we will wait before investing.

CHAPTER 30

Dividend Yield

The dividend yield is used to evaluate stocks we invest in for their dividends.

THE KEY IDEA OF DIVIDEND YIELD

The idea is to buy good businesses that are paying out consistent dividends at a good rate. The way to calculate a good dividend rate is to determine the *dividend yield.*

To calculate dividend yield, we compare the expected dividend per share to the price we are paying for the shares.

For example, if we are paying $1 for ABC shares and we expect ABC to pay out $0.10 of dividend per share per year, the dividend yield will be:

Expected dividend per share per year/share price
= $0.1 / $1.00 = 10%.

You have probably noticed that dividend yield is a way to calculate our returns on the amount of money we spent buying the stock.

There are a few things to note when using dividend yield to buy dividend stocks:

1. Check for consistency of dividend paid by the company. It should have been paying consistent dividends for the past 10 years for us to consider it as a stable dividend-paying company.
2. Aim for dividend yield that is much higher than the risk-free rate. Risk-free rates will be the higher of current bond rates or bank deposit rates. As a general rule of thumb, the dividend yield should be at least 2% higher than the risk-free rate.

CHAPTER 31

Growth Formula

Here is a formula that is not commonly known. We call it the Graham secret formula for growth stocks.

The Key Idea of the Growth Formula

The idea is that the PE ratio does not take into account the fact that businesses can grow.

Graham included an *expected growth rate* in the growth formula model in order to obtain an intrinsic value.

Here is the formula:

$$V = EPS \times (8.5 + 2g)$$

Where:

V is the intrinsic value;

EPS is the latest earnings per share;

8.5 is the assigned PE ratio of a stock with 0% growth rate; and

g is the expected growth rate for the next 10 years.

To determine an expected growth rate, we use the past 10-year growth rate.

If we use the example of Google, as at December 2018 we have:

EPS = $43.70

Past 10-year growth rate = 20.70%

Based on Graham's growth model, the intrinsic value of Google is as follows:

$V = EPS \times (8.5 + 2g)$

$V = \$43.70 \times [8.5 + 2(20.70)]$

$V = \$2,180.63$

We will add a 30% discount, known as a margin of safety, and we will get an entry price of $2,180.63 x 0.7 = $1,526.44.

PORTFOLIO

MANAGEMENT

CHAPTER 32

What Is Portfolio Management?

I have been invited to 24 different cities around the world to share my insights on investing. During this time, I've had the opportunity to speak to different people from all over the world. I always find it especially intriguing when I speak to stockbrokers. This is because regardless of where they come from, they all share a similar perspective. I remember the first time I heard a stockbroker in Cyprus give voice to it.

"When a customer opens a brokerage account with me, I can know within three months whether he or she will be a profitable investor."

"How can you tell?" I asked; I was curious.

"It's very simple. There are generally two types of investors: one that diversifies and one that doesn't. The one who does not diversify may make some money initially, but he or she loses it all eventually. Nobody can be right all the time. The one who diversifies will continue to survive long enough in the investment world to really figure out what is going on and start to become truly profitable. And within three months, I can easily observe which customers of mine have the discipline to diversify and which customers have a 'bet-it-all' gambling mind-set."

As my stockbroker friend from Cyprus said so well:

"Nobody can be right all the time." Hence diversifying our portfolio shows that we're humble and smart enough to give ourselves the right to be wrong and still have the ability to profit from our overall portfolio. Warren has an investment rule: "Never Lose Money!" This is not to say that we can never make mistakes in our stock selection, but we need to have a plan to account for possible mistakes and still be profitable overall.

In the next chapter, we will be sharing some specific ideas about how you can do that.

CHAPTER 33

Portfolio Management Rules

Have you heard the saying "Don't put all your eggs in one basket"? This speaks to the importance of diversifying our investments to manage risk, so that one disaster will not wipe out our finances. King Solomon, one of the richest and wisest people in history, advised us: "Invest in seven ventures, yes, in eight; you do not know what disaster may come upon the land" (Ecclesiastes 11:2).

Similarly, Warren Buffett once said, "Diversification is protection against ignorance." His portfolio contains more than 40 listed companies and hundreds of businesses privately owned by Berkshire.

I have made the mistake of putting all my investment money into one single stock, and then realized that even the best investment is never too good to fail.

So here are the key portfolio management rules that Mary and I suggest you adopt:

> Rule 1: Start with funds allocation.
>
> At any point in time, decide how much money goes into investments and how much is set aside as cash for future investment opportunities. This really depends on your assessment of how expen-

sive the market is at a given moment and how likely it is that a correction will happen soon. Typically, you should cast aside your own personal preferences and assess the economy objectively, as you would assess a company.

We can look at the PE ratio of the entire market and see if it is overvalued or undervalued. If it is undervalued, we can commit more of our funds to investing. If it is overvalued, we can set aside more cash in preparation for possible good opportunities when the market corrects. This was what Warren did in 1969 when he liquidated his money management pool, Buffett Partnership Limited, and stayed out of the market because stocks were overvalued. He then got back in four years later and described himself as being like "an oversexed guy in a harem." That move allowed him to avoid the crash between 1971 and 1974.

Rule 2: Never put more than 10% in any stock.

According to this rule, your portfolio should probably contain 15 to 20 stocks. "Wait a minute," you may ask, "shouldn't I have only 10 stocks since I will invest 10% into each stock?"

The rule is that your maximum investment in each stock should be 10%. And you should only commit the full 10% into those stocks that you have very high confidence in. This leads us to our next rule.

Rule 3: Stronger stocks, higher weight.

As we build up a list of stocks that we would like to purchase, it's a good idea to rank them in terms of how confident we are in their prospects. If we have a list of 20 stocks we want to purchase, we are bound to be more confident in some rather than others. You can either rank them from 1 to 20, or you can group them into bands or grades— e.g., grade A, grade B.

Realistically, we want to buy all grade-A stocks, but these stocks may not always be undervalued. However, when the right moment comes for us to purchase these stocks, it is only logical to commit more funds to them. For example, a grade-A stock may justify the full 10% allocation; a grade-B stock may justify committing only 9%, and a grade C, 8%. The underlying principle is to give higher weight to stronger stocks.

Rule 4: Review your portfolio at least once a year.

A commonly asked question is "How often do we monitor or review our portfolio?" Our suggestion is at least once a year. Companies listed on the stock exchange will issue their annual reports every year. Since these companies report on a quarterly basis as well, it may be a good idea to read through their quarterly reports to see how well they are doing. Typically, we will need to take note of any special situations and any news that the company announces that is out of the ordinary. If that happens, we have to ask ourselves if we still want to keep that stock. This leads us to our last point.

Rule 5: Do not sell purely based on price.

By this time, many investors will be asking, "When do I sell? What if the stock price rises or drops significantly?"

The answer to that question is to never base your decision to sell purely on price.

When we buy a business, we want to look at it as if we were employing this business to work for us in our portfolio. So the question will be "When do we terminate the services of this employee?" The answer will be "If this employee is no longer a good employee."

This means that we should review the business's performance together with its stock price.

WHEN STOCK PRICE DROPS

Suppose you bought a stock and the price dropped by 20%. You should not be in a hurry to sell it. Instead, you review the performance of the business. If the fundamentals have declined and you have lost confidence in the business, then you can sell it off. But if the long-term fundamentals are still great, you should not sell; in fact, you might consider buying more of that stock. Warren loves to buy stocks when their prices dip and he assesses their fundamentals as still being sound. American

Express was one such example. In 1963, the company experienced losses due to the salad-oil scandal, which left them liable for $60 million in damages. The share price fell from $65 in November 1963 to $37 in January 1964, a 43% decline in less than 90 days. Warren decided to buy shares of American Express, eventually injecting an investment of $13 million, which accounted for 40% of the then partnership's money. This initial $13 million investment in American Express has grown to be $14.4 billion today (March 2019).

WHEN STOCK PRICE RISES

Another scenario will be if the stock price suddenly increases significantly. There may be a temptation to sell off the stock and capture profits. Don't be in a hurry to do this and make the mistake of selling off stocks too early.

What should you do? You should review the business performance and revaluate the price based on the valuation methods discussed earlier in this book. If the business is performing well, you may not want to sell the stock because, based on the new valuation, it may be considered undervalued. In fact, you might choose to buy more of it.

But if you realize that the increase in price has caused the stock to be overvalued, you can sell it off to gain more cash and then buy it back later if the price falls.

It all goes back to fundamentals!

Remember: Benjamin Graham said that an investment is most intelligent when it is most businesslike. So think businesslike, and build a portfolio filled with great businesses.

CONCLUSION

CHAPTER 34

The Mind-Set of a Successful Investor

While I was serving in a military unit, my platoon regularly gave an award to the soldier of the month. On several occasions, the soldier who won the award was not chosen because of his strength, speed, or marksmanship. He was chosen because he had displayed the best attitude.

This is true for investors as well as soldiers. The market does not reward the smartest person on Wall Street. Even Sir Isaac Newton, a genius, lost millions in the stock market.

In an updated version of Benjamin Graham's *Intelligent Investor*, the *Wall Street Journal*'s Jason Zweig included a small anecdote about Newton's adventures as an investor in the South Sea Company:

Back in the spring of 1720, Sir Isaac Newton owned shares in the South Sea Company, the hottest stock in England. Sensing that the market was getting out of hand, the great physicist muttered that he "could calculate the motions of the heavenly bodies, but not the madness of the people."

Newton dumped his South Sea shares, pocketing a 100% profit totaling £7,000. But just months later, swept up in the wild enthusiasm of the market, Newton jumped back in at a much higher price—and lost £20,000 (or more than $3 million in today's [2002–2003's] money. For the rest of his life, he forbade anyone to speak the words "South Sea" in his presence.

If one of the smartest persons on earth could not beat the market, how then can so many others prosper?

Warren Buffett provided some insight into this conundrum when he said, "If calculus or algebra were required to be a great investor, I'd have to go back to delivering newspapers."

Peter Lynch, a legendary investor who made average annual returns of 29.2% as a manager of the Magellan Fund at Fidelity Investments between 1977 and 1990, said this: "Twenty years in this business convinces me that any normal person using the customary three percent of the brain can pick stocks just as well, if not better, than the average Wall Street expert."

We do not need to be geniuses to invest. In fact, many smart people are very bad investors because they rely too much on their intelligence. Ironically, the way to invest is to keep it simple.

This quote by Warren Buffett sums up this issue in an interesting way: "There seems to be some perverse human characteristic that likes to make easy things difficult."

In our journey as investors, we have seen work-at-home moms, taxi drivers, and factory workers build up substantial portfolios.

We make special mention of these groups because they generally have less money to save and fewer resources to begin with. But they are more successful investors than many wealthy individuals we know.

After spending time with so many investors, we have come to realize that the difference between a good investor and a bad one lies not only in the techniques each uses to pick stocks, but in the mind-set of the investor!

Here are some of the key characteristics that compose the mind-set of successful investors:

1. Patience

   In our journey as investors, we have met many people who crashed and burned their portfolio because of their quest to get rich quickly. But as Warren Buffett said: "No matter how great the talent or efforts, some things just take time. You can't produce a baby in one month by getting nine women pregnant."

   Impatience and eagerness to get rich quickly is the key cause of failed investments and people buying into scams that promise high returns. It is important to recognize and be aware of the need to be patient.

   George Soros said, "If investing is entertaining, if you're having fun, you're probably not making any money. Good investing is boring."

2. Independent thinking

   We have yet to meet an investor who got rich merely by following tips or hearsay. All successful investors practice independent thinking and are responsible for making the ultimate decision on whether to invest in a stock. This is sometimes known as contrarian thinking. A good example of it occurred in the late nineties when Warren refused to ride the dot-com wave, a decision for which he was ridiculed. In late December 1999, *Barron's* even published an article titled "What's Wrong, Warren?" which suggested that Warren might have lost his magic touch as the tech-heavy NASDAQ went up by 145% while Berkshire, adamantly holding on to its value stocks, was down 44%. And then, as we all know, the dot-com bubble burst. Being able to stand against the temptation to follow the crowd is the mark of a true contrarian investor.

As Peter Lynch said: "While some might mistakenly consider value investing a mechanical tool for identifying bargains, it is actually a comprehensive investment philosophy that emphasizes the need to perform in-depth fundamental analysis, pursue long-term investment results, limit risk, and resist crowd psychology."

It is very important to practice independent thinking and resist what is popular.

3. Focus

Another key characteristic of an investor is to be focused and not jump at every new idea.

Charlie Munger, Warren Buffett's business partner, said it well when he advised that "our job is to find a few intelligent things to do, not to keep up with every damn thing in the world."

A strong investor has to focus on what he or she

knows best. We have mentioned the circle of competence earlier in this book; it is very important to remain focused, and stick to it.

4. Consistency

We can see a lot of overlap among the characteristics. Being consistent is an important aspect.

The individual investor should act consistently as an investor and not as a speculator.

BENJAMIN GRAHAM

CHAPTER 35

A Game Plan to a
Multimillion-Dollar Portfolio

Congratulations on reaching this part of the journey! Having read the previous chapters, you have surely gained a lot of knowledge about investing. As the saying goes, "knowledge is power"; however, this knowledge will only remain as potential power until it is applied.

Mary and I have put together what we call the ideal road map to help you achieve financial success.

Here are the five steps you should follow in order to put what you have learned into practice:

1. Pay yourself first.
2. Save up for an emergency fund.
3. Get insurance.
4. Clear your debts.
5. Invest and compound.

Note that these steps can be done simultaneously.

1. Pay yourself first.

Start by paying yourself!

Most people tend to use their hard-earned monthly salary to pay their phone bills, utility bills, mortgages, transportation costs, food, clothing, and other necessities, and leave nothing for savings.

We suggest that you set aside a certain amount of your salary and pay yourself before paying anyone else.

We recommend that you set aside at least 10% of your salary every month. The more you set aside for your financial success, the sooner you can reach your financial goals. So get into the habit of saving cash as soon as you get your paycheck.

2. Save up for an emergency fund.

The first thing you should do with the money you set aside each month is accumulate cash for an emergency fund, also known as a rainy-day fund.

A good suggestion is to save up at least three months' worth of living expenses. If you need about $4,000 per month for basic living expenses, you should aim to save a total of $12,000 in your emergency fund.

So even if you lose your job, you will have enough money to tide you over for the next three months.

3. Get insurance.

Good investors should always prepare for the worst-case scenario. Many successful investors believe in the adage "Take care of the downside and the upside will take care of itself."

We should apply this wise advice to our finances.

A trustworthy financial consultant can help you find the proper insurance coverage. Anyone—even someone who is financially well off—can have their savings wiped out overnight due to a bad accident or health issue. It is imperative to have a holistic insurance plan to help you in case of need. Minimally, one should get an insurance plan that covers accident, critical illness, and hospitalization. Schedule an appointment with a trustworthy financial consultant to review your current coverage.

4. Clear your debts.

In addition to building your emergency fund and getting the right insurance coverage, you should settle any consumer debts you may have, such as those acquired through the use of credit cards. As we all know, credit card interest rates are much higher than the average, ranging from 8% to over 16% per annum. Pay off these debts and be free! If you have long-term loans, make sure the interest rates on the loans are as low as possible.

5. Invest and compound.

How much money can you save if you invest $100 per month? This depends on the returns you can get on your investment.

The following table shows several different scenarios for investing $100 per month at different rates of return.

In 30 years, you would have invested a total

amount of $36,000. Even at 5% returns, you would have accumulated $83,712.95. This is more than double the amount you have set aside.

If you apply the techniques of value investing wisely and achieve a return of 15%, you will have accumulated $599,948.30. At 30%, your investment will have grown to a whopping $13 million!

Many people wonder how Warren Buffett made billions. The answer is by being patient and by compounding!

Accumulated earnings with monthly investment of $100, compounded at various annual rates of returns		
Years	5%	10%	15%
1	$1,260.00	$1,320.00	$1,380.00
2	$2,583.00	$2,772.00	$2,967.00
3	$3,972.15	$4,369.20	$4,792.05
4	$5,430.76	$6,126.12	$6,890.86
5	$6,962.30	$8,058.73	$9,304.49
10	$15,848.14	$21,037.40	$28,019.13
15	$27,188.99	$41,939.68	$65,660.97
20	$41,663.10	$75,603.00	$141,372.14
25	$60,136.14	$129,818.12	$293,654.36
30	$83,712.95	$217,132.11	$599,948.30
	20%	25%	30%
1	$1,440.00	$1,500.00	$1,560.00
2	$3,168.00	$3,375.00	$3,588.00
3	$5,241.60	$5,718.75	$6,224.40
4	$7,729.92	$8,648.44	$9,651.72
5	$10,715.90	$12,310.55	$14,107.24
10	$37,380.50	$49,879.35	$66,486.42

15	$103,730.56	$164,530.26	$260,966.64
20	$268,830.72	$514,417.04	$983,058.12
25	$679,652.76	$1,582,186.78	$3,664,133.21
30	$1,701,909.46	$4,840,761.40	$13,618,777.35

If you can invest more than $100 per month, you can expect your investment to increase even more significantly.

Here is a table for a $200 per month investment:

Accumulated earnings with monthly investment of $200, compounded at various annual rates of return		
Years	5%	10%	15%
5	$13,924.59	$16,117.46	$18,608.97
10	$31,696.29	$42,074.80	$56,038.26
15	$54,377.98	$83,879.35	$131,321.93
20	$83,326.20	$151,206.00	$282,744.29
25	$120,272.29	$259,636.24	$587,308.73
30	$167,425.90	$434,264.22	$1,199,896.60
	20%	25%	30%
5	$21,431.81	$24,621.09	$28,214.47
10	$74,761.00	$99,758.71	$132,972.83
15	$207,461.11	$329,060.51	$521,933.29
20	$537,661.44	$1,028,834.09	$1,966,116.23
25	$1,359,305.52	$3,164,373.55	$7,328,266.42
30	$3,403,818.92	$9,681,522.80	$27,237,554.69

What if you're able to invest $500 per month?

Looking at the following table, we can see the possibilities! At a 20% annual rate, in 30 years, an initial investment of $100 will be worth $8.5 million!

Accumulated earnings with monthly investment of $500 compounded at various annual rates of return		
Years	10%	15%	20%
5	$40,293.66	$46,522.43	$53,579.52
10	$105,187.00	$140,095.66	$186,902.51
15	$209,698.38	$328,304.83	$518,652.78
20	$378,015.00	$706,860.72	$1,344,153.60
25	$649,090.59	1,468,271.82	3,398,263.80
30	$1,085,660.55	$2,999,741.51	$8,509,547.30
	25%	30%	
5	$61,552.73	$70,536.18	
10	$249,396.77	$332,432.08	
15	$822,651.28	$1,304,833.22	
20	$2,572,085.21	$4,915,290.58	
25	$7,910,933.88	$18,320,666.04	
30	$24,203,807.01	$68,093,886.73	

Your wealth will not grow unless you take the first step and start to save each month. Then watch and see what you can make happen.

We are so glad you have taken this first step of your voyage with us!

Epilogue

Congratulations, you have completed the entire book! We sincerely hope that it has given you insights on how to invest like a Buffett.

We recommend that you visit Mary Buffett's website at www.marybuffett.com, which has excellent blogs and articles.

If you really want to learn more about investing, the Buffett Online School provides an array of courses that teach you a proven, step-by-step method for planning your journey to financial freedom. Visit www.buffettonlineschool.com for more information

Good luck and we wish your prosperity in your investing journey.

Epilogue

ACKNOWLEDGMENTS

MARY BUFFETT

Sincere thanks to my children—Erica, Nicole, and Sam—for your constant love and support; Sean Weiming and the entire Buffett Online School staff; Success Resources Asia; my editor, Roz Lippel; and my friend and assistant, Jocelyn Skinner.

SEAN SEAH

My deepest gratitude to my friends who stood by me in this journey, Mary who is my mentor in investing and business, my family who gives me joy and strength, and my parents who always direct me back to God.

INDEX

accident insurance plan, 31
accounts payable, 117, 119
accounts receivable, 115, 142
accrual basis, 142
Allergan PLC, 82
Alliance Data Systems Corp., 83
Ally Financial Inc., 80
Alphabet Inc., 83
Altria Group Inc., 81
Amazon, 71, 98
American Express, 43, 75, 80, 166
annual reports, balance sheet notes in, 124
Apple Inc., 80, 81
assets
  accounts receivable as, 115
  on balance sheets, 111, 112–13, 114–17, 119, 120, 146
  business shares as, 133
  cash as, 115
  current, 112–13
  definition of, 111
  fluctuations in value of, 113
  inventory as, 115, 119, 120
  noncurrent, 112
  personal balance sheet example of, 112–13

balance sheets, 111–25
  assets on, 111, 112–13, 114–17, 119, 120, 146

basic questions answered on, 121–23
business example of, 113–21
business shares on, 133
debt evaluation using, 121–23
debt-to-equity ratio and, 123–24
definition of, 111
determining growth of business using, 121
equity on, 111, 113, 118
as financial statement, 108
investment checklist using, 139
investment decision and complexity of, 124
liabilities on, 111, 113, 117
net current assets on, 160
notes in annual report on, 124
personal example of, 111–13
as snapshot in time, 113
three main segments of, 111
two key things to look at on, 125, 139
understanding language of, 107–09
bank accounts, for emergency funds, 29
bank balances, as current asset, 115
bank loans, as current liability, 117
Bank of America, 80, 174, 175
Bank of New York Mellon Corp., 82

Index

Index

Index

Index

Index

Index